Additional Praise for Love Your Job: The New Rules for Career Happiness

"Millions of older Americans will have to work longer to achieve a secure retirement, but burnout can be a big obstacle. Now we've got a thoughtful, fun-to-read action plan for staying engaged and passionate about work from one of the best experts on careers after age 50—Kerry Hannon."

—Mark Miller, retirement columnist for Reuters, Morningstar, and WealthManagement.com

"Work should offer more than a paycheck. Work is also a big part of the daily search for meaning, the desire for a sense of fulfillment, the pursuit of community and connections. Kerry Hannon has written an indispensable guide for people looking to find or reignite purpose and joy in their job. *Love Your Job* reflects the wisdom she's gathered over the years interviewing, thinking, and writing about jobs and careers—insights she brilliantly translates into practical strategies for us to consider."

—Chris Farrell, author of *Unretirement: How Baby Boomers Are Changing the Way We Think About Work, Community, and the Good Life*

"Kerry Hannon demonstrates that loving your job is not a mysterious process, and it does not depend on the power or whims of others. She succinctly explains the specific set of behaviors, actions, thoughts, and beliefs that lead to meaningful job satisfaction now and in the future."

—Bruce Rosenstein, Managing Editor, Leader to Leader, and author of *Create Your Future the Peter Drucker Way*

"There's a lot to love about Kerry Hannon's *Love Your Job: The New Rules of Career Happiness*. It's a fresh and inspiring guide to recasting work into something that's meaningful and motivating. The result is a thoroughly researched and beautifully written book, putting solutions squarely in the hands of the reader with many practical ideas on making virtually any kind of work more engaging."

—George H. Schofield, PhD, author of *After 50 It's Up to Us*

Love Your Job

Love Your Job

THE NEW RULES OF CAREER HAPPINESS

Kerry Hannon

WILEY

Creative Director: Scott A. Davis
Cover Design: Lesley Q. Palmer Photograph: © Elizabeth Dranitzke, Photopia

Published by John Wiley & Sons, Inc., Hoboken, New Jersey.
Published simultaneously in Canada.

AARP produces print and e-books on a range of topics. Visit AARP.org/bookstore.

For general information on our other products and services or for technical support, please
contact our Customer Care Department within the United States at (800) 762-2974, outside the
United States at (317) 572-3993 or fax (317) 572-4002.

Wiley publishes in a variety of print and electronic formats and by print-on-demand. Some
material included with standard print versions of this book may not be included in e-books
or in print-on-demand. If this book refers to media such as a CD or DVD that is not included
in the version you purchased, you may download this material at http://booksupport.wiley.
com. For more information about Wiley products, visit www.wiley.com.

Library of Congress Cataloging-in-Publication Data:
Hannon, Kerry.
  Love your job : the new rules of career happiness/Kerry Hannon.
    pages cm
  Includes index.
  ISBN 978-1-118-89806-2 (paper); ISBN 978-1-118-89804-8 (ePDF); ISBN 978-1-118-89805-5
(ePUB)
  1. Job satisfaction.   2. Career development.   3. Employee motivation.   I. Title.
  HF5549.5.J63H276 2015
  650.1–dc23
                                                                    2014043441
Printed in the United States of America
10 9 8 7 6 5 4 3 2 1

For my mom, Marguerite Sullivan Hannon

Contents

Introduction   **xi**

    What My Dog Taught Me about Loving My Job   xi

Chapter 1 Curing the Workplace Blues   1
    Should You Switch Careers?   3
    Chin Up!   6
    Take It Up a Notch   7
    Loving Your Job   8
    The "HOVER" Approach   9
    Get a Grip   10
    How to Use This Book   12

Chapter 2 Creating the Blueprint for Your Dream Job   15
    Map Your Future   16
    Your Past Isn't Prologue   16
    Nothing Is Forever   18
    Look at the Big Picture   19
    What Would Make You Love Your Job?   21
    What Are Your Work Goals?   23
    Adopt New Ways to Envision Your Career   24
    Chapter Recap   27

Chapter 3 Do an MRI on Your Work and Your Life   29
    Create Your Job "Budget" Sheet   30
    What Does Your Work Really Mean To You?   32
    Write in Your Journal Every Day for a Week   35

Contents

Is Your Pay What's Really Bothering You?   38
A Can-Do Philosophy   38
Consider Taking a Self-Assessment Test   41
Get Ready to Love Your Job   44
Chapter Recap   44

Chapter 4   Refresh Your Attitude: The Keystone to Your
Love Your Job Action Plan   47
Attitude Adjustment   48
Create Your Own Purpose   49
Write It Down   50
A Picture Is Worth a Thousand Words   51
Build a Bear   51
Practice HOVERing   52
Mental Games   57
Adjusting Your Attitude   59
What to Do If You're Bullied at Work   60
Step Right Up and Enroll in My Three-Step Fitness Program   64
Chapter Recap   71

Chapter 5   Beyond the Job Description   73
Take Time for Renewal   74
Volunteering and Mentoring   77
Adding Value to Your Job   85
Take Control of Your Time   94
Get Involved in "Extracurricular" Activities   96
Chapter Recap   98

Chapter 6   How to Build Flexibility into Your Job   99
Work Flexibility and Happiness   100
A Myriad of Flextime Options   102
How Is Flextime Working?   104
Is Telework for You?   109
The Risks of Working at Home   111
Chapter Recap   119

Contents

Chapter 7 How to Upgrade Your Game   121
    The Benefits of Learning New Tricks   122
    Learning and Healthy Aging   123
    Getting Over the Hurdles   128
    Chapter Recap   135

Chapter 8 How to Have the "What's Next?"
Talk with Your Boss   137
    The Time Is Now   138
    Questions to Ask Yourself before the Big Meeting   140
    Your Plan-and-Prepare Strategy   142
    Carrying Out the "Ask"   146
    Chapter Recap   158

Afterword   161

Resources   165
    Ideas for Further Reading   165
    Helpful Career Happiness Web Sites   169

Acknowledgments   173

About the Author   175

Index   177

Introduction

What My Dog Taught Me about Loving My Job

All I really need to know about loving work I learned from Zena, my Labrador retriever. My resolution has always been to try as hard as I can to follow her example.

Start the day with gusto. Zena wakes with a mission. She's motivated. And she's determined to motivate me. She stands beside my bed, rests her head on the mattress, her eyes level with mine, and stares piercingly, willing me to get up.

She's always eager to face the outside world. In fact, she charges into it, and returns to dive into her breakfast with delight. Then she's ready for a vigorous workout to stay physically fit. That's a 40-minute-plus walk either around the sidewalks of the city or through the woods and fields, depending on where we are that day.

Focus on a task. Zena's singular ability to concentrate all her mental and physical energy allows her to achieve winning performance. She's a pro at what she does, and she devotes her whole heart and all her abilities to every project. She's absorbed with every sinew and nerve. She's vibrant and alive.

Throw a Frisbee, ball, or stick, and she's off, tearing down the field, knowing instinctively when to pivot and leap to catch it. She dives with abandon into ponds, and swims with the strength and pure beauty of a canine athlete, making a direct beeline to her goal in record time.

As far as I can tell, she never blocks out the pure enjoyment these moments offer by letting other matters distract her. Admittedly, she *is* free from worrying about finances, fitness, or health. Instead, she delegates those matters to me.

Stay present. Zena is wholly present, in the moment, with all her being—a state that comes naturally to her. Her attentiveness to what she's engaged in is never clouded by her future ambitions or the need to return e-mails, to tweet, or to juggle three jobs at once to keep her business prosperous.

Value yourself and charge accordingly. Zena doesn't do anything for free. She gets paid in the form of barter, of course, but she gets paid well for her services. There are no pay cuts, layoffs, or furloughs in her world.

She commands benefits we can only dream of scoring. Her bosses adore her. She knows this, but she doesn't take it for granted. She has a contract, albeit implied, that includes all-expenses-paid, first-class accommodations wherever she roams; high-quality and nutritious meals; vacations; spa treatments such as massages and pedicures; and other enviable employee fringe benefits.

Look at what goes right. Zena concentrates on the positive aspects of her job. She doesn't dwell on the negative or complain or whine about the long hours when she's parked under my desk while I work and her talents aren't being put to their best use. In a nutshell, she's optimistic.

Push in fresh directions. Zena is always on the lookout for new opportunities. She takes advantage of every walk. Smells and sounds lead her from one new place to another with openness and a fresh sense of excitement. She never fails to gain from social gatherings and networking events with her dog pals. She rarely turns down an invitation to a dinner party at our friends' houses.

She regularly keeps her skills sharp and adds new ones by attending training classes and workshops with internationally renowned dog trainers Jack and Wendy Volhard, authors of *Dog Training for Dummies* (Wiley, 2004), and participating in an engaging rally class that keeps her on her toes as she moves through a course designed to test her skills and obedience. Her goal? Progress, not perfection.

Network more. Zena may have a comfy job running our homes and lives, but that doesn't mean she stops networking. She's proactive about her networking efforts—attending events and reaching out to professionals in her field whose work she respects. She is always going out for walks to reconnect with longtime contacts, even those she has known since puppy kindergarten—anything she can do to keep old relationships solid and grab opportunities to build new ones.

Go places. Zena knows the importance of travel, of going new places and experiencing new sights, sounds, and cultures. Her official job title: Road Manager. We log more than 25,000 miles a year rolling from Washington, D.C., north to Pittsburgh, Philadelphia, New Jersey, Boston, and south to Virginia, South Carolina, and beyond.

Each time out the door, out of the comfort zone of her fluffy dog bed and the safety of her fenced yard, she learns valuable skills—and maybe even gets some insights into how to manage me better.

She trots out to the car and pops in without looking back. No questions asked. She props her front feet on the console of my Subaru Outback and stares fixedly out the front windshield as if asking, "What's next? Let's go!"

"By the way," she silently commands. "Can you roll the window down? I want to pop my nose out, feel the wind on my face, soak up the smells—and use all my senses to enjoy the ride."

Why the "lessons" from Zena? I share these teachings with you because whenever I feel lost, or resentful, or bored with my job, I look at Zena and remember that life is for enjoying and pushing boundaries and learning. She personifies the purity of loving your job. In the following chapters, my hope is that you, too, will experience a Zena-like "aha" moment and find ways to discover real joy in your own job. Let's go!

Love Your Job

CHAPTER 1

Curing the Workplace Blues

■ ■ ■

When was the last time you were so passionate about your work that it didn't seem like work at all? Or truly excited by all the new stuff you were learning on your job? Or genuinely couldn't wait to get up and head to the office because your bosses and colleagues were so much fun to work with? Has it been a while since you felt the eagerness and butterflies you had during your very first week at your job? Has that professional spark been doused, or is it still flickering, just waiting to be reignited?

Choose a job you really love and you will never feel like you're working another day. But what should you do if the thrill is gone? Is it really possible to get your groove back? Yes! What if you never had it in the first place? Yes, you can get in the groove.

If you're not there yet—and I assume you're not if you're reading this book—you've got company. About 50 percent of workers say they're unsatisfied with their jobs, and only 15 percent say they are very satisfied, according to a recent report by the Conference Board, a business membership and research group that has been conducting surveys about worker happiness since 1987.

Workers are least satisfied with promotion policy, bonus plan, training programs, performance review, and recognition, according to the most recent survey. Not surprisingly, high-income earners are more satisfied than lower-paid workers—and the gap has been

1

widening in recent years. The survey found 64 percent satisfaction among those making $125,000 and over.

Another dismal report was the annual Federal Employee Viewpoint survey, administered by the U.S. Office of Personnel Management. It revealed a federal workforce whose satisfaction on the job has steadily waned since 2010. The percentage of respondents satisfied with their jobs fell to 64 percent in 2014 from 72 percent four years ago. Pay satisfaction has fallen, too.

The latest declines, however, follow on the heels of a few years of federal employee pay freezes, along with higher health care costs tapping into paychecks. Not surprisingly, the survey also found that fewer workers would say their agency is a good place to work for anyone interested in joining the troupe. That number fell to 62 percent this year from 70 percent in 2010.

The fact is Americans are quitting their jobs at the fastest pace since early 2008. In October of 2014, 2.8 million people quit a job, the most since April 2008, according to the Labor Department's monthly Job Openings and Labor Turnover Survey, known as JOLTS that was released in November.

Millions of people currently in the workforce could use a little career boost to keep their work a source of enjoyment—for lots of reasons. While many people are comfortable with their current jobs, they may feel an underlying tension that they won't be prepared should a merger or marketplace change put their job in jeopardy. That anxiety may linger beneath the surface. Other people may work for a company that has gone through a period of cost-cutting, eliminating positions and suddenly leaving less room for advancement and growth. The path to promotion is not always there, or at least not clear. They feel like they're trapped in a dead-end job.

But just saying "take this job and shove it" is probably not the best approach to battling your boredom or pent-up frustration. Quitting is generally not a good option, unless you already have a new position lined up elsewhere or you already have the means to retire—in which case, lucky you.

If you're tempted to quit without a safety net, keep in mind the statistics: In the United States, unemployment generally lasts around 50 weeks for workers over 55 and 30 weeks for workers under 55, according to the Bureau of Labor Statistics. And a recent report by the International

Labour Organization, a UN agency, stated that "in many advanced economies, the duration of unemployment has doubled in comparison with the pre-crisis situation," referring to the global economic downturn that exploded in 2008. The average length of joblessness, for example, recently hit nine months in Greece and eight months in Spain.

So no, you don't necessarily want to just throw in the towel on your current job. But don't worry. The truth is that finding happiness and fulfillment in the workplace doesn't always mean a big swerve from the past, or starting from scratch in a new job or career. It does, however, often call on the courage to make necessary but sometimes uncomfortable and even painful changes. You may need to take a long, hard, honest look within yourself to figure out what's holding you back from making modifications to your current job.

Love Your Job will show you how.

You may need to engage in some thoughtful sleuthing and inner soul-searching to figure where you can uncover new challenges and opportunities in your working life. You may need to dig deep down to tap the energy and determination needed to make the necessary moves. But even small ones have the potential to deliver big rewards. If you really want to love your job, you must first be able to step back and appreciate what's going right about it, even if there are times when you dread that upcoming assignment, meeting with the boss, or lunch with a difficult client.

You'll need patience, because change doesn't always happen on your time schedule. But you also need to start the ball rolling, even if just a little bit at the start.

In the following pages, you will learn ways to do just that.

Should You Switch Careers?

I'm a big advocate of following your heart to do work that you love, and I've written extensively and speak frequently about career transition to audiences around the country. Many of us at this time in our lives feel the allure of a career switch to follow a dream, often one from childhood, or to find work with meaning and purpose. When things go sour at work, many people imagine starting over in a second act or a new career to pursue a long-standing passion. They fancy it will be their magic elixir.

And it can be. In my book *What's Next? Finding Your Passion and Your Dream Job in Your Forties, Fifties, and Beyond,* I highlight stories of people who succeeded at doing just that. If you're thinking along those lines, I support you, but be aware: Most of those people work harder than they ever have. Still, they find that it's worth it, and they love what they do.

Here's the truth: In recent months, I have found through hundreds of meetings, interviews, and consultations with people seeking career advice that the big shift isn't always practical for many people—regardless of how miserable they are in their jobs. It's not that there isn't the will. But when it comes to the way, there are sobering stumbling blocks. Inertia can hold you back. The fear of failure when you make a big career shift and begin all over again in a new field can be paralyzing.

And at the heart of it, the biggest roadblock is money. Not having employer-provided health insurance and retirement benefits is a genuine concern. Then too, when you start over in a new field, particularly if it's a nonprofit, you can generally expect to earn less, at least initially. And when you go the entrepreneurial route, you may need to forgo a salary entirely for a year or more until your business gains traction.

When I press people who seek my advice on what they really want to do with their work lives, I have found that many people don't actually feel the urge to make a huge career shift. They kind of like their job, and they just need to get their dance back.

And this is what I tell them and what I'm telling you: You *can* fall back in love with your job again, even if you've been doing it for decades. And if you never loved your job in the first place, I can help you find ways to enjoy it more—or at least like it enough to take some pleasure in it. Many paths can lead you to this place. You can discover how to make old workplaces feel fresh, and learn ways to raise your hand that will open doors to new experiences and career moves. It's never too late to make your job a source of joy, as well as a paycheck.

DO I REALLY HATE MY JOB? OR IS IT BURNOUT?

Job burnout is far more than just feeling trapped and uninterested in your work. New research from jobs site Monster.com finds that a staggering four in five workers experience burnout at their jobs.

According to the Mayo Clinic, "Job burnout is a special type of job stress—a state of physical, emotional, or mental exhaustion combined with doubts about your competence and the value of your work."

The clinic's web site has a list of questions to help you decide if you're experiencing job burnout. Here are some of them:

- Have you become cynical or critical at work?
- Do you drag yourself to work and have trouble getting started once you arrive?
- Have you become irritable or impatient with coworkers, customers, or clients?
- Do you lack the energy to be consistently productive?
- Do you lack satisfaction from your achievements?
- Do you feel disillusioned about your job?
- Are you using food, drugs, or alcohol to feel better or to simply not feel?
- Have your sleep habits or appetite changed?
- Are you troubled by unexplained headaches, backaches, or other physical complaints?

If you answered yes to any of these questions, you may be experiencing job burnout. Be sure to consult with your doctor. Some of these symptoms can also indicate certain health conditions, such as a thyroid disorder or depression, according to the web site.

Plenty of factors can trigger burnout. They include a sense of powerlessness to influence decisions that affect your job such as your schedule, assignments, or workload; not having the resources you need to do your work; and working with an office bully or a micromanager boss. If you feel isolated at work, you may feel more stressed. If your job is monotonous, that can push you over the edge, too. And of course, your work-life balance could be out of whack—too much work, not enough life—which I discuss in later chapters.

(continued)

Burnout can result in a multitude of medical problems, from fatigue and insomnia to depression, anxiety, alcohol or substance abuse, and even heart disease and a vulnerability to other illnesses, according to the Mayo Clinic's medical experts.

Chin Up!

Trust me—I know how easy it is to complain about a job that's flat-lined or a bad boss. I've done it myself. But it never makes the situation better. Ever. So stop it right now. No one really cares about your kvetching. They will listen politely at first, but then you become nothing more than a tiresome broken record. Whining is not the path to career happiness. The squeaky-wheel approach? Yes, that can work. But just complaining and not doing anything? Forget about it.

If you want to be happier, you have to do something, to take action. "Speak now or forever hold your peace," as my dad always said. In other words, get that hand waving wildly in the air and make some noise.

Here's another analogy that works for me, as an equestrienne: Say I'm cantering toward a jump on my horse, and I keep missing the proper distance to ask her to jump from. At times like this, despite more than four decades of competing at the top tier of the sport, I'm generally feeling defeated in my ability to ride successfully. I fight back the urge to blame my horse for not responding properly to my leg and hand signals, or my trainer for building a jump that is just too difficult for us. Still, I get frustrated and angry with myself, and I'm filled with the impulse to give up.

That's when my trainer says, "Why not make a different turn to the fence, change your approach, plan a different path?" It comes down to a subtle shift in how I navigate, and perhaps a slight adjustment in pace. Only a real aficionado of the sport would discern it, but inevitably, when I heed my trainer's advice, my horse and I find the perfect spot and we take flight. I smile. Job well done. I can't wait to do it again.

What I am driving (or galloping) at here is that you have to learn to focus on remedies, not faults. It's hard to act. But once you have a plan, you'll be surprised at how empowering it can be.

Take It Up a Notch

Love Your Job is about raising your game with your current job and finding value and meaning in the work you do week in and week out. But finding ways to love your work entails taking ownership of your life. No one is going to wave a magic wand for you. You may have to take a risk. And nothing happens overnight. In essence, you need to constantly ask yourself, "What can I do to improve myself on the job?" not "What can my boss do for me?

A 58-year-old producer at *60 Minutes* recently told me that while he loves producing great documentaries for a primetime news show, he is well aware that his field is in flux. To keep fresh, every year he sets himself a goal—to learn someone else's job, add further skills, study something new. "For example, this year I'm going to learn how to edit in my spare time," he says.

He has to carve out the time to take on the new goals, but it's mentally engaging and gets him out of his comfort zone. It also allows him to have a better appreciation of the work his coworkers perform and builds a sense of camaraderie when he asks them to teach him. He assures them he is not trying to wrest their job from them, or become an editor, but simply to learn more about the process. At the very core, it can create new friendships at work, but that's not all. "I guess the best part of it is that I get a kick out of learning something new that helps me do my job better," he says. "I love that."

That's the approach I want you to take. My goal is to provide you with the tips you need to thrive in your current work—to build new outlooks, find satisfaction around the edges of your daily duties, and craft a more entrepreneurial attitude toward your job. I will show you ways to examine your job responsibilities, your work rituals, and your attitudes toward your work. And I will show you how to ask the hard questions: What new habits or routines can you craft to bring more love to your workday? What inner changes can you make to rekindle your hope, eagerness, and resilience? How can you learn to celebrate even your smallest successes?

In the process, you will glean how you can identify what makes you feel good about work, and how to recognize the negative thoughts that creep up in your loop of self-defeating talk. You will learn that by truly looking someone in the eye, listening, and supporting your colleagues and championing their successes, you can renew your own energy, gain confidence, and build the resources to face new challenges.

My approach is a positive, can-do look at work that offers creative solutions. Bottom line: You will find novel ways to design your job around love. This is a book about taking control of your own workplace happiness, but it's grounded in the real world. This is not pie-in-the-sky conjecture. These are actionable steps.

Loving Your Job

I believe you really can learn to love your job. I do. I'm a romantic that way. Love is a complicated thing. It can be fleeting. You have to give it to get it. And at times it takes effort to hold on to it. At the heart of it, a job, like romance, is never utterly full of bliss and joy.

Sometimes work is like climbing a mountain, says Dan Ariely, who teaches psychology and behavioral economics at Duke University. This is how he explains it: When you're on your trek, it's cold. You're physically exhausted. But you care about the fight, the challenge, and when you come back down, you want to do it again. All kinds of things can motivate us to work, he says. But Ariely has found one thing is clear: Like mountain climbing, when there is some effort involved, most people love it even more.

What doesn't motivate us is the Sisyphean horror of pushing the same boulder up the same hill over and over, he points out. That's the essence of doing futile work, says Ariely. We all need some sense of progress. It's demotivating just doing the same thing again and again.

What it means to love your job is a mash-up of effort and joy, good days and bad days. That said, researchers studying the application of positive psychology to the workplace concur that a positive mind-set affects our attitudes toward work as well as the results that follow. In the following chapters, I hope to inspire you to focus on your strengths, to give yourself credit—even for small successes—and, yes, to be grateful. These are essential ingredients to being happy at work. You will discover the best ways to fight back against the stress, anxiety, and even boredom that any job can sometimes involve.

The "HOVER" Approach

In Chapter 4, you will discover the core elements that comprise my HOVER approach to revamping your work life. The acronym HOVER involves looking down, surveying the situation, and then strategically employing the five basic ingredients you need to create the change you're looking for—hope, optimism, value, enthusiasm, and resilience. (See "The HOVER Approach" sidebar.)

You will see firsthand how others have made these changes. You will learn from interviews with leading workplace psychologists, career coaches, experts on positive psychology, and professors at leading universities around the world about why having an open

THE HOVER APPROACH

HOVER stands for the five core ingredients you must have, or will need to develop, to create change in your working life.

- **Hope** is essential. When you have confidence that you can reach your goals, you will find a way to do so.
- **Optimism** allows you to have a positive approach, which helps you keep pushing ahead even when there are roadblocks.
- **Value** means knowing that you have something to offer— the skills and talent to get results and make progress, if you put out the effort.
- **Enthusiasm** is the intangible "oomph" factor that provides the energy needed to make those necessary changes, both internally and externally.
- **Resilience,** the knack for springing back in the face of adversity or failure, is indispensible to achieve happiness at work.

mind and always looking to learn something new, to take up professional development and training opportunities, and to face other challenges will keep your work fresh, meaningful, and moving forward—regardless of your age or the stage of your career.

I have found through my research that many midcareer workers tend to avoid new challenges on the job or assignments that feel like a stretch. They worry too much about whether they have the skills needed to take on a loftier new role. They fret about failing, so they cling grimly to doing only what they are already know and feel comfortably safe performing. When offered an opportunity, they fall back on the excuse that they're unfamiliar with that kind of work or that it isn't what they went to school for. I advise them to shift from thinking "I'm not ready to do that" to thinking "I want to do that—and I'll learn by doing it."

Love Your Job will encourage you to be more open to taking risks at work. Allow yourself to fantasize about your career, to really soul-search. I believe we all should have long-term aspirations of where we would like to be in a year, two years, and five years. Pursuing flexible workplace goals that you set for these predetermined time periods will help keep you motivated as you learn new skills and take on new challenges.

Get a Grip

As New Agey as it sounds, you will also learn that part of loving your job involves loving yourself and paying attention to your body and your soul. To love what you do each day, you need to be physically, spiritually, and financially fit. Think about it: How many times have felt that you are running so fast that you barely have time to think? How often do you actually allow yourself to pause and listen to what your body, your heart, and your mind are telling you?

Talk with enough happy workers and you'll find that the secret is feeling in control: having a job that offers you a bigger say in what goes on at work, more flexibility in scheduling day-to-day activities, and more opportunities to pursue professional passions and develop new skills. Increased autonomy, too, will frequently lead to increased satisfaction. I'm reminded of the poem "Invictus" by the English poet William Ernest Henley, which I have been told Nelson Mandela, who was imprisoned for 27 years, had written out on a scrap of paper. The last two lines of "Invictus" read, "I am the master of my fate, I am the captain of my soul."

Be patient—it can take a little time. But "find a way," as the 64-year-old endurance swimmer Diana Nyad said after completing her inspiring swim from Cuba to Key West, Florida, on her fifth try. In September 2013, Nyad swam 110 miles across the fearsome Florida Straits in just 52 hours and 54 minutes—the first person to do so without fins or a shark cage.

"It's not so much the physical," Nyad told the Associated Press a day after finishing her record-setting swim. "To my mind all of us . . . we mature emotionally . . . and we get stronger mentally because we have a perspective on what this life is all about. It's more emotional. I feel calmer. I feel that the world isn't going to end if I don't make it. And I'm not so ego-involved: 'What are people going to think of me?' I'm really focused on why I want to do it." Her message: "Never, ever give up."

Nyad's inspiring comments tell me that you can't get caught up in the drama and emotion of what's holding you back from finding happiness in your work. You can't act based on what others expect of you. You can't do a job simply because it's someone else's vision for you, or you're worried about what others will say if you make a move to a new department or want to step back from some of your duties to find more balance in your life.

This is *your* life, naysayers be damned. Who cares if someone says you're foolish to want to swim with sharks, if that's the goal you've set for yourself? What matters is why *you* want to do it. It's virtually impossible to make a big life change, or stretch for a new goal, if you're doing it for someone else's approval or respect, or worried what others might think.

The only way I've been able to make a major transformation in my life, whether job-related or personal, is to do it for *myself.* Not for Dad, or my spouse, or my best friend, or even my career coach. You have to do it for yourself. That and only that will make the process meaningful and give you the chops to ride it to a successful conclusion, even though you may very well experience setbacks along the way. This is life, after all. Nyad can tell you all about that.

How to Use This Book

Love Your Job is designed to show you how to make the best of your life and your career. It will help you get reinvigorated about your job. In these pages, you'll discover the ultimate guide to making your job a great one. I'll give you the action steps to take to make your job work for you. I'll deliver the professional advice and strategies I've been doling out as a career transition, retirement, and personal finance expert and journalist for more than two decades. Each chapter will conclude with a short recap and action steps to keep you working toward your goals.

I have arranged this book so you can dip in and out of the chapters as they apply to your situation. You'll find tips on how to renew your working life by getting involved with special projects, mentoring, meeting new people, asking for new responsibilities, finding work-life balance, and adding skills, training, and education. You'll learn how to think like an entrepreneur while working for someone else, have the "talk" with your supervisor or the human resources department, and make a sideways move and look for opportunities within your company.

Here are a few suggestions to consider before we start:

- You do have ways to change your job, but remember: The goal that is most important to you today may very well change to another down the road. You might have several aspects of your job that you'd like to change. That's all well and good, but focus on the small wins. Skip the big, bold goal. Don't try to do everything in one fell swoop.
- Start by doing one small thing that matters. When you move in small, incremental ways, you will have a fighting chance of getting your changes approved and set in motion. Truth is, sometimes all it takes to right your ship is that one special tweak.
- That said, if you're one breath away from quitting your job because you hate your immediate boss, drastic action might be required. (You probably won't be surprised to learn that the main reason people quit is an unbearable boss.) At the very least, you need to pause, review, and try to get some clarity. You might need to reach out to human resources for guidance. See my section on how to deal with bullying in Chapter 4.

- My three-part fitness program (see Chapter 4) will help you prepare for making changes in your work and your attitude. You will discover why it is essential to be physically fit, financially fit, and spiritually fit to face the stress and demands of making changes in your career.

I wrote this book to help you find the work you love. Life is too short not to spend your time making a difference and finding meaning and joy in your daily work life. So let's go for it!

2

Creating the Blueprint for Your Dream Job

■ ■ ■

To find out what will make you love your job again, you need to do some homework. It all begins with some inner soul-searching. The best way to get down to the nitty-gritty is to pull out a notebook, or open a new Word document on your computer, and devote it to your Job Remodeling project. I find that the process of writing these things down in a journal gives them meaning and a focus that you can't get by talking about it. Meantime, it allows you to capture a snapshot of your job that's hard to get any other way.

This is your personal journey, so store the information in a safe place. By keeping the journal private, you're free to write without feeling that someone is judging you. This is your vision. You may want to share it with a career coach or a consultant down the road to help you draw conclusions or develop an action plan.

As management consultant Peter Drucker wrote in his book *Managing in the Next Society*: "The most effective way to manage change successfully is to create it."

To go from merely surviving in your job to thriving, you need to find meaning in your work or to accept it for what it is—a paycheck—and stop complaining. (I hope you don't fall into this latter category.)

My goal for this book is to provide an interactive path for you to start your passage to a happier work life that is more than an income. The simple action of putting it all down and letting it out provides clarity. You begin to connect the dots and see how you can tackle the issues and find solutions.

Map Your Future

"It is not unusual for a career coach to start with someone who is blocked, hates their job, and feels totally trapped," Beverly Jones, an executive coach at Clearways Consulting in Washington, D.C., told me. "One thing that happens lots of times is people do the same thing for too long. And they start to become preoccupied with the things they don't like. They want something fresh, but they feel stuck. That's why they come to coaching."

The first thing Jones does is to ask people to break their job and their life into pieces. Instead of saying, "I hate this, I can't stand this, I can't take it anymore," she asks her clients to simply write a list describing the three big parts of their lives *outside* of work: their fitness, their spiritual life, and their social life. "Many times, what people say is, 'I don't have a life because all I do is work.' Put these elements down anyway, even if you don't," says Jones.

In essence, you create a map, she says. "You identify the pieces, and you create a strategy for each of the pieces."

AARP's Life Reimagined web site (lifereimagined.aarp.org) offers an entire section devoted to creating a LifeMap. "You are the artist of your life" is the theme. Users are encouraged to picture the things they want to achieve in their work and their personal life. You select images that represent the future you want for yourself—accomplishments, work, personal, financial, relationships—even pulling from pictures you have posted on Facebook.

It comes down to a process of reflecting on your strengths and weaknesses to help you understand your past and present selves so you can see what needs to be changed down the road.

Your Past Isn't Prologue

How do you describe your job right now? Is it "work"? An avocation? A calling? A mission? A passion? A chore?

When I think of my job, it's both a passion and a mission. Underneath that overarching description, there are lots of moving parts. On one level, my job, like yours, is made up of the process of my work, all the things I do that I get paid for, the specific tasks. The physical, tangible results I produce are another aspect—the joy of the finished product. Next, it's how it makes me feel inside. And, finally, it's the impact it has on others, the very rewarding feedback I often get.

Fill in this sentence in your journal: "My job is my . . . ." This isn't a timed test. So think about it and truly take the time to describe why you define your job by one or more of the terms above. Can you provide examples of something you have done at work that fits the description? What are the areas in your work in which you are a star?

Then tackle this sentence: "My job consists of . . . ." Don't make this a bland job description. Instead, think of the skills you use each day, the activities you participate in, your responsibilities. Try to be active in your language, such as managing people, solving customer problems, writing fundraising grant proposals, organizing meetings, fixing computers.

Don't dismiss the window-dressing. On a superficial level, a "job" is embodied by the specific words you use to describe what you do. For me, my various titles include author, editor, columnist, reporter, speaker, coach. Of course, we all know that our title or our place in the hierarchy doesn't come close to defining our job in all of its aspects.

These words have psychological repercussions. For many of us, our job designation gives us a sense of pride, and that definitely falls into the pot of things you love about your job. Being a vice president, say, or a manager, or an executive producer has a nice ring to it. As you move up in your career, those monikers do mean something. They are our badges of accomplishment and recognition.

What's your title? What's your dream title? Write that down, too.

And we all know that our job is not just an eight-hour stint. For some people, it's *always* on our minds. It's in our inner psyches. We carry it around with us. We worry about it. We work out problems even when we aren't at our desks. We stew over conflicts with coworkers over the weekend. We look forward to new projects in our downtime.

Truth is, smartphones make it really hard to step away from many jobs for long. And if you love your job, that's cool. If you don't, you're in trouble.

Our jobs identify us to the world around us, too. Whether you're at a party, or meeting someone for the first time at a charity event, or at one of your kid's soccer games, chances are the question "what do you do?" pops up. It's an integral part of our social persona.

What do you say when someone asks you what you do? Does it make you uncomfortable? What would be your ideal response? Note that in your journal.

Write a short personal mission statement. In a few key sentences, sum up what you really want in your job. If you can do it in one sentence, all the better.

Make a list of what job success and job happiness mean to you.

- Is job success a priority in your life?
- Is it more important than being a good parent?
- Is it more important than being healthy?
- Does making a great income motivate you?
- How critical is the respect you get from your coworkers?
- Does knowing you are always learning new things bring joy to your job?
- Do you value making an impact through your work on other people's lives or the environment?

One recent Saturday, for example, I stopped to chat about work and jobs with Jamie Rappaport Clark, whose son, Carson, rides horses with me. "I love my job because I love our mission," she said with a smile. She has spent three decades working in the field of conservation, and it still lights her up. Jamie is president and CEO of Defenders of Wildlife, a leading force in the protection of wildlife and wild lands. Jamie beams when she talks about her work and shrugs off the political tussles, long hours, and extensive travel involved. She knows she's making a difference.

Nothing Is Forever

A job is ever-changing. Over time, we're assigned a series of job titles, as our roster of responsibilities morphs. What you love about your job right this minute is probably not what you will love about it next year, and certainly not precisely what turned you on a decade ago.

But my theory is that the spine remains the same. Your core skills and interests remain at the heart of it, but the moments shift that make it bright, as you learn and add to your core skills. I like that. The fact that our jobs keep changing challenges us. It keeps us from getting complacent, stuck in a rut, taking things for granted.

But for many people, that excitement gets lost somewhere along the way. Changes don't turn out for the better, or perhaps the job really is repetitive and dead-end. Getting sucked into a mindless routine deadens you inside and puts you in jeopardy of losing your job if your boss notices. When you lose pride in what you do, your health, your personal relationships, and your sense of self-worth begin to diminish. And then perhaps the day comes when you can barely get out the door to get to the office.

Put simply, you tune out. You don't tap into the energy that can come from your job, or you simply can't begin to see where the hope lingers below the surface. In fact, just 30 percent of employees in the United States feel engaged at work, according to a 2013 report by Gallup. Around the world, across 142 countries, the proportion of employees who feel engaged at work is just 13 percent. That's discouraging. But you don't have to be one of them.

Look at the Big Picture

Let's start to work through what would make your job loveable. It's critical to appreciate all the things that make up your job. Most jobs are multifaceted, which is great in many ways. You wear lots of hats. As companies have downsized to become leaner and survive, workers are stretched not only to do the job they were originally hired to do, but those once done by coworkers who are no longer on the payroll as well.

Then, too, it may have always been that way. If you work for a small company or a fledgling nonprofit, your ability to be a jack-of-all-trades is why you were hired in the first place. Such opportunities can make work interesting, but they can also be overwhelming at times. After running flat out, you burn out.

So turn it around. When one part of your work is not going swimmingly, more than likely there's another bit that's still feeding your creativity.

In your journal, make a list of all of the things you love or ever did love about your job, the things about your job that make you feel alive, or used to. Allow yourself to see the entire picture of your work. Don't dwell on what's going wrong or making you feel powerless.

Here are some thoughts to get you started: What you love might be special assignments that take you out of your comfort zone. The best jobs are, to be honest, the ones that scare us a little at times. You get smacked with stomach-churning dread that you might fail. Admit it—there's a jolt of energy from nerves, and when you succeed, it's a high. These emotions might bubble up because you've been asked to meet a tight deadline for a project, or have to speak in front of an audience, or lead a meeting, or create a marketing plan for a new client.

But you might love the fact that sometimes your job is so engrossing that you forget what time it is. You are one with the work. But when our jobs start to weigh on us, it's easy to forget that we once enjoyed magic moments like that.

The times at work when you can freely take your foot off the gas might be something else that scores high on your list of things you love, or used to love, about your job. Employees who take a break every 90 minutes report a 30 percent higher level of focus than those who take no breaks or just one during the day, according to Tony Schwartz, the CEO and founder of the Energy Project and bestselling author of *The Way We're Working Isn't Working: The Four Forgotten Needs That Energize Great Performance* (Free Press, 2010).

Schwartz's firm partnered with the *Harvard Business Review* to conduct a survey of more than 12,000 mostly white-collar employees across a broad range of companies and industries. Employees who took the break also report a nearly 50 percent increase in their capacity to think creatively and a 46 percent higher level of health and well-being

Does your work have meaning to you? Note this in your journal, too. Employees who get meaning and significance from their work were more than three times as likely not to change employers, according to the Energy Project findings. These workers also reported 1.7 times higher job satisfaction and they were 1.4 times more engaged at work.

Does knowing your boss has your back make you feel good about your job? Feeling cared for by a supervisor has a major impact on how people feel about their job, according to the study. Employees who say they have more supportive supervisors are 1.3 times as likely to not quit and are 67 percent more engaged. Sometimes it really is all about the boss. A 2014 global workforce study by the consulting company Towers Watson of 32,000 employees found that only slightly more than half of employees say their leaders inspire them and make them feel energized about their work.

Thirty percent of employees report a lack of supervisor support such as a lack of recognition and feedback, and managers not living up to their word as a cause of work-related stress.

Now let's dig even deeper. What's the essence of loving your job? Is it a feeling that you are in control of your destiny to some extent? Is it having autonomy and flexibility in your schedule? Is it knowing that you really do have the chops to do your job?

To begin the falling-in-love process, you need to be psychologically ready for the changes you want to make, too. It's quite possible that you will grieve for what you are leaving behind when you start to move the pieces around, particularly if you're seeking big changes in your daily routine and responsibilities. When you lose the security blanket of doing what you already know you can accomplish, you may long for the comfort of the good old days.

As you begin to fill your journal, imagine that you are the architect of your career. You *can* transform your job into one you love. This is your blueprint, and it's a work in progress.

What Would Make You Love Your Job?

Creating a job you love can mean moving to a different department, even on a temporary assignment, or getting involved in an industry group in your after-work hours. It could be mentoring someone who may not even work for your employer. It might be taking the time to do things that don't necessarily relate to your day-to-day activities on the job, but can have the power to positively impact it, if word about your activities trickles back to your boss through the pipeline. Being valued by industry peers outside of your regular office environment, for instance, can send a message back to the home base.

One of the real reasons I have found that people often fall out of love with their jobs stems from a lack of the human touch—connecting with colleagues, bosses, and even the mission of their employer.

Consider how you communicate at work. Do you fire off e-mails and texts and rarely speak to someone in person or on the phone? Do you make a point of stopping by someone's office just to ask how it's going? Do you see colleagues outside of work? Are you brusque and all business when you're in the office? Or do you let aspects of your inner personality show? Do you wear your passion for your work on your sleeve? Do you really listen to other people? Are you present?

If you can find ways to communicate your own passion and energy and interact with others at work, chances are new invitations, opportunities, and projects will crop up.

HOW TO FALL IN LOVE WITH YOUR JOB (EITHER FOR THE FIRST TIME OR AGAIN)

Here are some suggestions from Dan Schawbel, best-selling author of *Promote Yourself* and *Me 2.0*:

- Master your current role and then find creative ways to expand it so you can best leverage your strengths and passions while supporting your company.
- Spend more time with people at your company you haven't worked on projects with or had lunch with before. This way, your work environment will become fresher and more interesting.
- Find the things that you love about your job and put more energy into them.
- Learn a new skill or topic that will help enhance your job and make you more productive.
- Volunteer for a committee or special-interest group at work so you become more involved and better networked.

What Are Your Work Goals?

We all have widely varying goals for what happiness at work means. Enter these targeted goals on your blueprint. Here are some to consider to get you started:

I want to . . .

- Be assigned projects that challenge me and make me feel energized.
- Learn new skills.
- Have a more flexible work schedule and more control over it.
- Cut out the commute and work from a home office.
- Feel like I have job security.
- Find ways to stand out and be unique and get promoted.
- Work in a less stressful environment.
- Ease off the fast pace, by traveling less on business or working fewer hours.
- Find more camaraderie and a stronger sense of community.

Each of these goals will vary depending on who you are and what you need and want from your job. Cherry-pick the goals you want to work on today, and remember that it might be something else a year from now.

Some possible ways to meet these goals include switching departments, having a conversation with your boss about changing your workload, getting involved with a mentoring program or a special project, and even asking for a raise. Yes, money matters when it comes to loving your job. Let's not be "holier than thou" here. Sure, you can be passionate about your work, but if you aren't paid what you feel you're worth, you will never be truly happy. Scoring more pay can be self-affirming and a sign that your work is valued.

Money may be all you need to get a boost of energy and excitement about your work again. But getting up the nerve to ask for a salary bump can be agonizing. You will learn more about these specific actions in future chapters. For now, you can begin to work on your inner game. You do have control over your workplace—or at least the way you feel about it.

Most of you probably like your field, or you wouldn't have started down that path in the first place. And my guess is you don't need to "reinvent" yourself to find happiness at work. What you need is to find ways to redeploy or hone the skills you already have, to add new ones, and to open your eyes to new opportunities.

Adopt New Ways to Envision Your Career

One of my favorite visualization exercises is to imagine a career as a jungle gym, not a ladder. This is my favorite tip from Facebook Chief Operating Officer Sheryl Sandberg's wonderful book, *Lean In*. Maybe that's because when I was growing up, I loved playing on the jungle gym.

To me, it's a great image of the twenty-first-century career path. "Ladders are limiting," Sandberg writes. "Jungle gyms offer more creative exploration. There are many ways to get to the top of a jungle gym. The ability to forge a unique path, with occasional dips, detours, and even dead ends, presents a better chance for fulfillment."

In essence, you might have to reach down or over in your company's organization to find work you love. Sometimes a lateral move to gain knowledge and experience across business lines is a better option than a promotion within your current department, and it can help you dodge being promoted up a silo by bosses using your talents to advance their own careers.

Maybe it's not the money but rather climbing the ladder that will make you happy. Maybe a more prestigious title resonates with you. Then again, maybe neither of these things will make you love your job. Some people simply don't want more accountability, greater responsibility, and the added work hours that inevitably come with them.

I'm well aware that that sounds somehow politically incorrect. We've all been trained since birth to climb, climb, climb—to reach for those lofty goals and brass rings. But I believe joining the race is way overhyped as a sure route to happiness. And as people get older, I've seen that it grows less and less important in the grand scheme of things that matter in life.

Advancing to a job you love might mean accepting less pay and even a title that isn't as prestigious, or one that is out of the limelight. It's your "inner job" that I'm advising you to explore. People who truly love their jobs often talk about aspects of their work that have little to do with themselves. When I ask people what they love about their work, they often say something like, "Good people work at my company. I love my department and the people I work with every single day." Let your internal compass lead you to a job you love.

HIRING A CAREER COACH

A big reason many of us feel lost in our work life is that we can't imagine what we really want to be doing, what we have a passion for doing, in this chapter of our lives. So we freeze in place.

If you know you need an adjustment but are uncertain of what to do, a career coach can help you set goals, outline the moves you need to make, and motivate you—if it fits in your budget.

Sure, you can ask your friends, family, and colleagues past and present for advice, but often I find it helps to get unprejudiced guidance from an outsider who can focus just on you and your unique set of circumstances.

A 2014 study by the International Coach Federation of 18,810 workers representing 25 countries found that the number one reason cited for seeking coaching was to enhance work performance (42 percent), followed by expanding career opportunities (33 percent), increasing self-esteem/self-confidence (31 percent), improving business management strategies (29 percent), and managing work-life balance (27 percent). Interestingly, men were more likely than women to receive coaching to expand professional opportunities, while women were more likely than men to seek coaching to improve work-life balance.

Hiring a coach can be a little tricky because there are so many people out there who call themselves career coaches. Your employer might offer coaching as a benefit, so check with your human resource department or your supervisor. Another place to look for coaching help is at the alumni office of your alma mater. Local libraries and community colleges frequently offer coaching workshop sessions, too.

One place to start looking online is the Life Planning Network (lifeplanningnetwork.org). This web site offers a directory of

(continued)

coaches geared to midlife workers. You might also want to tap into expert mentor advice via PivotPlanet (pivotplanet.com). I have found the experts there to be very knowledgeable, even during a one-time visit, and you can hire them as coaches if you choose.

Here's how to pick a coach:

- *Seek out credentials.* Career coaching is a self-regulated profession. It's not essential that your coach has a professional designation, but it's an indication that he or she has taken the time to undergo formal preparation and follow general standards of professionalism. One place to find a directory of credentialed coaches is the International Coach Federation (ICF; coachfederation. org). ICF-credentialed coaches have met educational requirements, received coach training, and undergone a number of experience hours, among other requirements. Two other helpful sites are the Association of Career Professionals International (acpinternational.org) and the National Career Development Association (ncda.org).
- *Do your due diligence.* Find out as much as you can about the coaches you are considering and their own career journey. What led them to coaching and what kinds of workers have they helped to date? Do they have any specialty? Most coaches have web sites that can help you with this background check. Search the coach's name on the Web. You can find coaches who have a blog via directories such as Alltop.com (careers.alltop.com)) or who are on Twitter by searching WeFollow under #coach.
- *Request references.* Don't expect that checking references will reveal any dirt, but it will give you an opportunity to find out more about any potential coaches, how they like to work with clients, and, importantly, what worked in their sessions with the coach that solved their issues.
- *Look for a coach you can meet with in a way that works best for you.* You might opt to meet in person, on the phone, by e-mail, or by Skype or Google+ Hangout. You don't need

to work with a coach who lives nearby. The key is to have someone's undivided attention. So if your friend has a great recommendation for someone in another state, you can work with that coach, too.

Once you've narrowed your search, you may want to connect with a few candidates to find one who fits for you. The initial meet-and-greet session should be free of charge. Even if your most trusted colleague loved the coach, it will come down to how you personally connect with him or her. You'll be revealing intimate details of your life, your dreams, and your strengths and weaknesses, so you'll want to feel safe and be able to trust that person completely.

Ultimately, the career coach you hire should encourage you, drive you, and give you the inner confidence to step into the untried with grace. But it won't work if you aren't in sync and open to the help.

Rates will vary—anywhere from $50 to more than $200 per hour. Some may want you to agree to a minimum number of hours. A typical coach-client relationship lasts from six months to a year.

That said, you might start with one or two meetings, or weekly or monthly meetings. And you have to be accountable for actually making active changes. I love it when coaches give homework to prepare for future sessions, or suggest books to read. Assignments keep you working toward your goal of changing your work life for the better.

Finally, remember to treat your relationship with your coach as a business one. Your agreement will spell out what you expect from the coach and vice versa.

Chapter Recap

In this chapter, we've begun the preparatory efforts needed to find happiness at work. To thrive, review your life both inside and outside your job. When you clearly define and choose your goals, you begin to put your new job in motion. Meanwhile, you can take action steps today to start that internal change process.

Your To-Do List

- Begin a journal in a notebook or computer file for your "Job Remodeling."
- Write down in your Job Remodeling journal your career and personal goals and other information prompted in this chapter.
- List dream jobs you would love to have.
- Make a list of people you know who love their jobs, and ask them what they love about their work. It can inspire you.
- Write down the times in your life when you loved your job, and why.
- Consider and, if appropriate, look into opportunities for career coaching.

3

Do an MRI on Your Work and Your Life

■ ■ ■

I t's not cool to complain.

It's remarkably easy to fall into the trap of whining and grumbling about a boss, coworker, or employer, but it rarely makes things better. For some people, it's standard practice. It's a rote response you get when you ask them about their job. They roll their eyes and wearily spout out something derogatory. But, frankly, it's self-defeating. It saps your energy, and honestly, those around you grow weary of hearing it.

Get over it. Do something. Change comes from within. No one is going to do it for you. As the ubiquitous Serenity Prayer says, "Grant me the serenity to accept the things I cannot change, the courage to change the things I can, and the wisdom to know the difference."

That means you have to look underneath the lid to get down to your center and take inventory. You need a clear vision of what would make your job better for you. It's up to you to unearth the ingredients that will create a solution to your current unhappiness or boredom. I'm not saying everyone can find that solution where they work right now. But you need to try, and you need to be willing to make compromises.

Changing jobs is not a great option for many of us in our 50s and up. Our salaries are too hard to replace at another employer. Our age is a red flag for many employers, even if no one wants to talk about it. It's reality. And while starting over in a new career or starting up your own business may sound dreamy, it is daunting, and not everyone is suited for that kind of big shift. The grass is not always greener. Trust me. I have interviewed hundreds of people who have changed careers and am well aware of the challenges they faced, both personally and professionally.

In other words, suck it up.

The symptoms of job distress are many and varied, and they're hard to break free of once you're lost in the downward spiral. Often, the very atmosphere at your workplace feeds on it, if one employee after another is griping about his or her situation, too. It's poisonous. You have a pit in your stomach when you think about heading to the office. You find yourself approaching your projects with indifference. You sigh when given a last-minute assignment that needs to be done ASAP. You resent your workload or the fact that you're not getting promoted the way you once were.

Stop the looping chatter. You're in a rut. Let's start by doing a full-body scan to determine what it is you're longing to get from your job.

Will a bigger paycheck make you whistle while you work? Will psychological rewards—more pats on the back? Would flextime make the difference, or less travel? Is it a more simpatico band of colleagues to bond with and share challenges?

No two people are looking for the same ingredients, so there is no cookie cutter solution to what will make you love your job. There's no "one size fits all." It's your own recipe. But there are steps you can take to break free of the malaise.

Create Your Job "Budget" Sheet

Conduct an honest appraisal of your skills and interests. Write these down in your journal. Much of what you already know is transferable to your next undertaking with your employer and with your job. The key is to match your job or career to your innate talents and personality.

Write down the key areas in your life that matter most to you. For example, you might list the following concepts:

- Inner peace
- Family and friends
- Career satisfaction

- A loving relationship
- Travel
- Financial security
- Hobbies
- Keeping fit and healthy

Write down an assessment of who you are:

- Are you an introvert or an extrovert?
- Do you enjoy working on solo projects or on teams?
- Do you benefit from brainstorming sessions or do you shut down and retreat?
- Are you a self-starter or do you perform better when you work with a manager to monitor your progress and keep you accountable?
- Do you get bored easily?
- Are you creative?
- Are your organized?
- Do you thrive on structure?

What are your goals? We covered these in a quick hit list in the previous chapter. Review them and build them out in this section. Try to be as specific as possible. This is your opportunity to be candid about your goals, who you are, and the things you love. When we tell someone of our ambitions, or at least put them down on paper, they become real, and we can begin to gradually find ways to incorporate them into our daily lives.

Next, look back at what you said you like about your job right now. Trust me, there are some things. Do you like your coworkers, your work schedule, your salary, the respect you get from your boss and your peers?

Now assess what you don't like. Let it fly. This can be a cathartic exercise. You're bored. You're doing the work of three people. You have repeatedly been overlooked for promotions. You're tired of the relentless travel. Your boss is a total jerk. You don't like the hours.

Not every job is picture-perfect or one you will love every day, but when you create a job budget sheet—what I call the "Love Your Job Budget"—you will begin to see plainly how you can balance the assets and liabilities of your work life to produce a positive "net income" that adds up to loving your job most of the time. At its heart, this exercise lets you create the "pros and cons" list of your current position. Remember when you were a kid, and your parents told you to write out the pros and cons? I do. It helps.

Once you see your entire job in black and white, it becomes tangible, and you can start to discover ways to trim back the problems of the job—the liabilities and debts, to stick to the financial analogy—and add steadily to the positive net income aspects of your work.

On the plus side, for instance, you might put down what you have been successful at in the past or what makes you laugh at work. Do you like not having to work on the weekends? Do you have some hidden talents or desires you've never revealed to your manager that might be worth exploring? Adding new activities to your current job, maybe something as simple as enrolling in a yoga class offered at your company's fitness center, might be enough to help you transition to a better outlook on your workday.

My "Love Your Job Budget" is a process that will develop and morph over time. But once you get started, you will find that it will give you an outline to follow, with immediately actionable steps and others you can add on as you go. Like your monthly household budget, you will want to review it every few months to see where you need to tweak it. And when a major life event occurs—an illness or an unexpected financial windfall, perhaps—you will find ways to adjust your goals and your action plan to suit your new circumstances.

Falling in love with your job will take effort, especially if you have been at a company for a decade or more. It's tough to break old habits or to change your supervisor's perceptions of you as an employee. Good relationships take work. Even the best marriages and partnerships go into a slump if they aren't nourished and tended to on a regular basis. You've got to keep things fresh. The bottom line is that you must commit to working on your Love Your Job Budget every day. Are you willing to do this?

What Does Your Work Really Mean To You?

Often, it begins with an acceptance of balancing needs and wants in our entire lives. "When clients come to me and says they are unhappy in their job, what I usually do is sit down for a 'getting real' talk with them," says George H. Schofield, a career expert and psychologist. He asks: "Where are you in your life? Why are you working?" The truth is, for many people it might not be so much about falling in love with the work itself, for example, says Schofield. It's loving what that work does for them in other areas. A 59-year-old, for instance, might be continuing to work for the health care benefits. Or it might be a lifestyle choice. "I have a client who loves to ride horses. She works mornings in a call center because that way she has her afternoons to go to the barn."

When she said she was unhappy at work, Schofield asked her *why* she was working. "I know you aren't happy with your supervisor, who is a real micromanager," he said. "But in the end, how much can you do about that? You only work four half-days a week and your have the rest of time for your horses. Isn't that enough?"

So what is the match between why you're working and what it's delivering to you? "I would love for everyone to love their job," Schofield told me. "But could we get real here, please? You have to take a look inside and see what your motivations for work are and what needs your work is meeting."

I love Schofield's "warts and all" approach, and I agree with him in many ways. Once his horse-loving client put it in perspective, her attitude improved, and she was able to focus on what she gained from the arrangement. She homed in on the positive elements of her job and the freedom it ultimately gave her, and learned to cope with what she couldn't change—her boss's management style. She was able to stop letting her boss make her crazy by visualizing her time spent at the barn as the carrot, so to speak.

As Schofield puts it, there are people who depend on their work for their "OKedness." It's how they identify themselves, and it is imperative that they love their work because it is who they are. They are generally happy with their work, and when things get rocky, they instinctively find ways to fix it. It means too much to them to approach their job any other way.

There's also a group of people who just work for the fun of it. They're not doing it for the money alone. It's something that really engages them and feeds them creatively. They also tend to have few complaints about their positions.

But lots of people fall somewhere in the middle, like Schofield's horse-loving client. It takes a "get real" evaluation to find out what's bothering them and what they can do personally to find a happier approach. And often it comes down to a trade-off. Once you accept that deal, you can quit wallowing in feeling-sorry-for-yourself mode, or being angry.

"I know in my own life I really love my work, but the real earthquake in my life was when I awoke one day, and I realized it was no longer about climbing the ladder for me, or getting another title or validation," Schofield told me. "My relationship to my work changed."

Is it realistic to expect your work to meet all your needs? In truth, it isn't all about the job. It's about something at a much higher level," Schofield says. "It is unlikely that you will love your work every day. But you don't have to actively dislike it. What's really important to understand is that your relationship to work changes, and work takes a different place in your life as you get older—particularly if you're no longer working for proof of your success."

So in this introspective stage, ask yourself, "What am I really getting out of work? Where am I likely going to be five years from now?" Life has a way of rearranging these things for us, but it helps to have a vision to guide you nonetheless.

WHY DO YOU WORK?

In working with clients, Schofield has identified seven reasons people work:

1. They work for identity.
2. They work for meaning.
3. They work for community.
4. They work for engagement.
5. They work for money.
6. They work for the benefits such as life or health insurance.
7. They work for validation.

Write in Your Journal Every Day for a Week

Now that you've looked at your job, your personality, and what matters to you from a broad perspective, it's time to get down to reality. Doing so will help you tease out precisely what it is about your work that's making you miserable on a regular basis. What are the things that you enjoy? I doubt you're going to love your job every hour of every day, but you really should be on board with it most of the time.

The best way to go about this process is to spend a week or two tracking your feelings and observations from the time you get up until the time you turn out the light next to your bed. Make note of what happens each day, how you feel at different times, what makes you smile and what makes you anxious. Jot down those moments when you feel confident and those when you feel bored, or stressed, or overwhelmed.

Be as precise as you can. If you can't isolate what it is that is at the root of your unhappiness, you won't be able to get to a better place. The bottom line: "If you're really unhappy at work, you can either find a way to live with it or you can come up with a strategy to change it," says career coach Beverly Jones, whom we met in the previous chapter. "There is nothing else. Those are the two things."

YOU'RE NOT ALONE

Root Inc., the strategy execution consulting firm, conducted a survey called "America's Workforce: A Revealing Account of What U.S. Employees Really Think about Today's Workplace." The survey asked more than 1,000 employees in the United States what they would like to see change at the companies they work for and the leaders who manage them.

Among the survey's findings:

- *Employees feel discouraged.* More than half (54 percent) have felt frustrated about work.
- *Manager/employee relationships need improvement.* Only 38 percent of employees strongly agree that their manager has established an effective working relationship with them.

(*continued*)

- *People don't understand strategic direction.* Fully 40 percent of employees say they don't get the company's vision or have never seen it.
- *Innovation is being stymied.* Nearly 67 percent of American workers can name at least one thing that would prevent them from taking any kind of risk at work.
- *Big picture contributions are missing.* Only 43 percent of workers say they feel accountable for the company's revenue, profit, or growth.
- *Managers aren't leading by example.* Just 26 percent of workers strongly agree that managers embody the values they expect from their employees, only 39 percent say their manager understands their role at the company, and only 40 percent feel strongly that their managers understand their company's strategy or goals.
- *Collaboration across teams is tough.* Just 27 percent strongly feel they can depend on outsiders to fulfill their duties when working with other groups.
- *Training isn't relevant.* A quarter of employees report they don't have any training available to them right now, and the 62 percent say they do have training available but believe it is either not at all or only somewhat applicable to their jobs.

The study also revealed some upbeat news and opportunities for companies to make changes:

- *Finding the bright spots.* Fifty-six percent of workers feel their company is better at identifying what works well than they are at fixing processes that are not working.
- *Training can make a difference.* Workers with training that is applicable to their jobs and is available to them feel more committed, happy, and excited about work than do those who did not have such access.
- *A glimmer of hope.* Forty-three percent of workers said they felt happy about work at some point in the last month.

"From connecting everyone in the organization to the strategy of the company, to creating the right culture that supports the behaviors and processes that will achieve the strategy, to making training more relevant to the jobs that people have, there are clear, actionable approaches that leaders can take to transform their organizations," said Rich Berens, Root president. "The good news is that while it's not easy to drive culture change or approach communication in a different way, it's all possible, and every incremental change will yield significant results."

So, say that you write down that your hours are really long, and it's a killer for you. That's something you can probably change. "There are people with more demanding jobs than yours. CEOs, the president of the United States—all kinds of people have found ways to attack the problem of hours," Beverly Jones, the career coach, says.

First, observe how much time you spend at work, and determine if you're wasting time. For now, just get it down in your journal. You'll want to see if there are things you can take out of your job, tasks you can delegate or that you can get more efficient at.

You may ultimately want to renegotiate the hours you spend on the job. But start with yourself. Deal with the things you can control. See if there are ways you can be working smarter.

If you're feeling totally bummed out and overwhelmed, get that down in your journal. Are you wasting lots of time? Look around and see if there are areas in your life where there is a lot of clutter. When people feel low on energy, often it's because they're not clearing out as they go. Their inbox is overflowing. Their desk is a disaster. Their file drawers are jammed. Even their garage is a jungle.

There is something about the activity of uncluttering that is liberating and empowering. "It's partly the process," says Jones. "It's the distinctions you're drawing. You are saying, 'This is valuable, this is not.' It's a physical, practical way to engage in making decisions about your life and what you want to do with it."

If you can get a serious clutter-clearing process going and you're letting go of stuff, you also tend to let go of a lot of your boredom and bitterness. "Engaging in getting rid of stuff brings a new perspective," says Jones.

Here's another typical example—your journal reveals that just don't like your boss. It happens. And it's not a comfortable thing to admit or to live with day to day. But in truth, there are things you can do to make it better. You might not be able to change your boss, but you can change how you view him or her. You can learn to be more compassionate if they have flaws. You can learn to communicate more effectively.

Is Your Pay What's Really Bothering You?

Research suggests that if you get a bonus or a big salary increase, the happiness impact doesn't last very long. "It seems to be important, though, that your pay is equitable," says Jones. If part of the reason you hate your job is you're paid way too low, you have some options. You could look for another job. You could find a side job. You could have that "talk" with your boss.

"If you feel you're getting paid less because you are a woman, for example, then that's a thorn in your side," Jones says.

A Can-Do Philosophy

When you read back over your journal, you'll find your problem areas and then, instead of saying, "I hate this," you'll be able to use this as a jumping-off point to ask, "How can I change this? What do I want to replace it? What's my goal?

My dad, who was my hero in so many ways, had a core can-do philosophy. Whenever I asked his counsel about a goal I had, he would always ask, "How *can* you?" even when others were telling me I couldn't do it. He never once doubted that I could.

And then he and I would break it down into steps for making it happen. He always said you have to dream to get there. And sometimes that meant dreaming of a better job and work life. I admit that one time when I laid it all out for him, he did advise me to quit. And three days later I did. I never looked back and am thankful for that move.

I started my own business, with my ex-employer as one of my new clients. But not everyone is hardwired for that kind of big change. And it did take several years to build my income stream back to where it was. Luckily, I had a partner, my husband, who was working full time and could provide ballast.

But I stuck it out for most of my 20-plus years of working in-house —although I always did writing gigs on the side to help balance any unhappiness and keep me stretching in new directions, building my network, and allowing me to feel less dependent on one employer controlling my destiny.

At various junctures, though, it really made career sense to move up and out, particularly when I got married and moved to a new city. That's far easier when you're young and beginning your career. When you're in your 40s and 50s, you need to keep your traction as best you can, especially in a job market that makes it tough for older workers to get hired.

For me, what worked for those times where I had to stay put, bide my time, and make it work was to take the feeling of being blocked, or being afraid of changing something, or trying to reach for a higher bar, and break it down into manageable parts that would make the job more challenging and affirming, step by step. I will elaborate on ways to do this in upcoming chapters.

So start small. Do one thing every day to move the ball forward. The first step in your change process: keeping your journal. It's simple stuff like making lists, for example, as you have already started to do.

Here's your homework, some of which you may have already begun in Chapter 2:

1. *Write out your "best of all worlds" list.* Start by creating a picture of what you desire in your work life. Be bold and think big. List the elements you already know you want in your work. Try to imagine a clear—but realistic—outcome, and list the precise pieces that make it so attractive to you.

   Create a section in your list for what you like best about your job right now. As I said before, I know there are things. Nothing can be that bad.

   I'm a big believer in positivity. Focusing on the positive gives us the strength to tackle the tough elements. I realize that we often become so discouraged by our current job demands that we lose touch with the best facets of our present work.

You might need to set aside time to calm and clear your mind before you do this exercise. Meditate, if that helps. Go for a long walk with your dog. When you're ready, consider features like:

- Your coworkers
- Interesting and stimulating work
- Opportunities for learning
- Occasions for networking
- Respect, cachet, perks, and benefits

Write your current job description as if you were telling a friend about what your duties are each day.

2. *Make a list about what you dislike in your job.* Then, one by one, consider what you can do to turn the negatives into positives. Reframe them. "If what you like least about your job is the stress, ask yourself what it is that might make the job less stressful for you," suggests Jones. "Regular vacations? No weekend work?"

Make a to-do list of the tools you will need to make these improvements. For starters, you will need to be physically fit. As you will read in the next chapter, this is key to making changes in your life. When you're in shape, you have vitality and energy that you can translate into action steps in all facets of your life. And it gives you a positive attitude. Fitness and health build confidence. You feel good. Then, too, stretching your brain, keeping your skills sharp, adding new ones, and meeting new people will help you push out of your narrow rut and see a bigger, brighter future.

3. *Track your progress.* If you're like me, you love crossing action steps off your to-do list. That's why it's great to mix small steps with bigger ones. By tracking your progress, even if this means checking off that you shined your work shoes (appearance matters in how you feel) or walked for a mile or two each day, or whipped up that banana-kale shake for breakfast, you can keep yourself accountable. There will be plenty of other such items on your list as you move through this

book. "Logs can illustrate your efforts, reinforce your commitment and help you see the gap between where you are and where you want to be," Jones advises.

In addition to both a daily and monthly to-do list, I recommend keeping a separate journal for musings and self-reflection. This private outlet encourages you to dig down and unload frustrations, vent, dream a little, and explore ideas and hopes no matter how high-flying they may seem at the time.

Finally, remember that this is not a task. Once you get started and make keeping lists and journaling part of your daily routine, it doesn't just give you a strategy for changing your work life, a structure, and a process. It has the added benefit of being energizing. It's your own personal business plan. That sense of taking control is empowering.

Consider Taking a Self-Assessment Test

Do self-assessment tests help? I get asked this all the time. If you are heading down the path of self-evaluation and peeling back the layers of your own personality, it's a good question to ask. The key to any of these personality tests is developing self-awareness. Having a sense of how your personality contributes to your happiness or unhappiness in your job is essential.

I have found the Myers-Briggs test (myersbriggs.org) somewhat useful. But I always feel a little frustrated because I don't believe that I fit into the test's specific categories, even when they are all mashed together. We all think we're special, after all.

You may have taken the Myers-Briggs Type Indicator at some stage—two million people take it every year—so you may know what I mean. It's a sort of gold standard of psychological assessments, and droves of employers use it when evaluating job candidates and more. The idea is that that each of us fits 1 of 16 personality types.

More than 10,000 companies, 2,500 colleges and universities and 200 government agencies in the United States reportedly use the test. An estimated 50 million–plus people have taken the Myers-Briggs personality test since the Educational Testing Service first added the research to its portfolio in 1962.

The core idea is that when you know your personality type, it will help you relate more effectively with your colleagues and better recognize your strengths. The test is often used to help pinpoint potential career fields, too.

The testing process is simple: a multiple-choice questionnaire, with a discussion afterward about what your personality type says about you.

The test can be helpful in a couple of ways. If you're an extrovert, you get your energy from other people. It's really important for you to be energetic in your work and to be interacting with other people. If you have a job that isolates you, you can suddenly have an "aha" moment and realize that's why you have been so unhappy. To fix it, you can look for ways to get energized by joining committees, volunteering, and getting involved with other people.

If you're an introvert, you might find constant interaction with other people to be exhausting. The test can help you figure out that you need to seek out ways to restore your energy by time alone at the office. Look for projects that involve independent research.

These kinds of assessments can also help you learn how to communicate your style with other people. Maybe you're a "big picture" type, and you find it boring to go step by step. That might be why you're having so much trouble communicating with a boss who goes step by step. By seeing that, you can learn that you're going to have to compromise. Knowing that about yourself can really help smooth your interactions.

The Myers-Briggs assessment costs $15 to $150, depending on the depth of the test and how fast you want the results interpreted. Additional guides and tool kits rapidly increase the cost. The only way to take the test is through a certified administrator. Your employer's human resources department might provide the test. Many career coaches also now offer the service. If you are in the United States, an advising or counseling service at a local university or college may be able to suggest a person in private practice in the community who uses the test.

You can also find Myers-Briggs professionals in your geographic area through the referral lists on the MBTI® Master Practitioner Referral Network (mbtireferralnetwork.org), and the Association for Psychological Type International (APTi). In addition, APTi chapter leaders can suggest people in their areas; contact information for APTi chapters is also on the APTi web site (aptinternational.org).

If you are not in the United States, you can find a distributor in your country through the CPP (cpp.com) web site. CPP licenses the international distributors worldwide who provide Myers-Briggs training, translations, and support materials. Contact the distributor in your area and ask if a representative will assist you in arranging to take the test. If there is no distributor in your area, contact the MBTI publisher at globalsales@cpp.com, who will be able to help you.

You can also take the Myers-Briggs assessment and receive your results and interpretation assistance online. The MBTI®Complete is an online option from CPP, and individuals can take the test directly and review the results without a Certified Practitioner as the administrator. The web site is MBTIComplete.com.

Ben Dattner, an organizational psychologist and the founder of Dattner Consulting, recommends the Hogan Personality Inventory (hoganassessments.com). Unlike the Myers-Briggs, which provides an "I'm OK, you're OK"–type report, the Hogan Personality Inventory, he says, tries to identify themes like whether you're set in your ways, likely to get angry easily, or take criticism too personally. Once you recognize these personality traits, you can begin to accept your own role in why your job is a mess and begin to adjust your own reactions, rather than blindly blaming your boss or your coworkers. Gallup's StrengthsFinder 2.0, created by Tom Rath, is also a popular tool.

A further approach I find intriguing, if perhaps scary, is a 360-degree process where you get feedback from your boss and the people who report to you. This is something that an outsider, such as a career coach, will execute for you. You can learn a tremendous amount about your role in your company and how people perceive you at work. That certainly can be extremely revealing and give you tools to make internal and external changes.

But this one can be a little tricky because your boss, and sometimes supervisors higher up in the organization, has to sign off on it, and it can reveal information you might not be psychologically prepared for. You might ask for the comments to be anonymous, so if criticisms emerge, you won't be resentful or bear a grudge.

Get Ready to Love Your Job

In the end, however, after all the list making, self-evaluation, and dreaming, you have to *choose* happiness. Chances are, once you complete your MRI, you may land on one aspect of your job and yourself that's all encompassing and becomes the axis your job happiness will revolve around. It's the linchpin that will make change possible for you and keep you motivated to do the work needed to change the parts of your day-to-day work that need revamping. For the horse-loving client of Schofield, her centerpiece was a flexible work schedule.

But for many people, at the heart of it is *purpose*. As Jamie Rappaport Clark of Defenders of Wildlife told me with passion, "I love the mission of what I am doing."

"People want to do something they're proud of. They want to create something," Jones says. "They want to feel like they are helping other people. They want to be contributing to the community. People in nonprofits or government service seem to think they have the corner on that market. But I would say that people who work in business are as least as likely to believe in their mission—and in some cases even more. They feel like they are creating a product that makes a difference—say, a pharmaceutical that's saving lives. They work for a utility and are proud of how their company gets out and gets the lights on again after an ice storm."

If you're doing a job that you really don't believe in, you either have to find a way to make a positive contribution, or you're just going to have to leave," she concludes.

Chapter Recap

In this chapter, we've expanded on your self-evaluation of your working world and done the homework needed to create a detailed picture of it. You've built out your starter lists of what you love most about your job, the trouble areas, and your dream goals. This has been your deeper dive. You've reviewed personality assessment tools and learned about timely strategies career coaches say can help you create a better job for your future.

Your To-Do List

- Ask people you know who have had setbacks at work how they navigated rough patches to create a job they love.
- Continue journaling and writing to-do lists. Create a "job budget" and tweak it as you begin to take actions and get a clearer image of what you must do to change things.
- Track your progress, both the big and the small action steps you take toward your future.
- Take a personality assessment test, if that appeals to you.

4

Refresh Your Attitude: The Keystone to Your Love Your Job Action Plan

■ ■ ■

P assion and love for your work is the ideal scenario and something we all aspire to. But to be realistic, not everyone gets that opportunity—at least not all the time. Sometimes we get paid to do work that we're skilled at doing, even if it isn't our dream job. Sometimes we work at a job because there's a demand for it and we need the income. There are bills to pay.

That's why I cringe when I hear the cliché, "Love your job and you'll never work another day in your life." It's just not always attainable for everyone. And even if you land that perfect position, whether you're designing landscapes, building houses, doling out financial advice, or performing hip replacement surgery, you can feel lost, unchallenged, and unhappy at times.

If you have ever been in this situation, you know there's no easy panacea. But one thing holds true: The job is what *you* make of it. The challenge is to recognize what's troubling you and learn ways to push through the "woe is me" doldrums and to find ways to accept and understand why you're doing the job you're doing right now and make it work *for you.*

It's far too easy to fall into the "I'm a victim" mentality. You blame your unhappiness on a horrible boss, the long commute, corporate downsizing, or a myriad of other external factors. That default thinking is simply unproductive.

When it comes to action steps you can take to make your job better, it starts with you—even if you truly do have a horrible boss or a long commute.

In this chapter I make the case for changing your attitude—hitting the refresh button. It's my "starting from the inside" solution. And it requires adjusting your "inner" approach to work, your mental game. After all, your attitude is your keystone—the central piece that holds everything together.

In the following chapters, I'll lay out external strategies to make your job a whole lot better, such as asking for new responsibilities or learning new skills, getting involved with special projects, adjusting your workday, mentoring, nurturing relationships, or meeting new people. But let's start by exploring what you can do all by yourself *without* having to get your boss on board, at least not yet. How you feel is something *you* can control. If you can master these tweaks, many of them subtle, it will make a huge difference in how you approach your job.

Sweeping actions may not even be entirely necessary if you take the time to address your inner game and your personal goals. At the very least, if you can begin to find ways to psychologically experience your job in a more positive way each day, you can buy yourself some time to put the broader changes into play.

Bottom line: Regardless of the external trappings of your day-to-day responsibilities, it's how you feel *inside* that matters.

Attitude Adjustment

It doesn't surprise me that coach Beverly Jones, introduced in Chapter 2, says the number one reason people come to her for coaching is boredom. They don't describe it that way, she says. They complain that they feel stuck. They feel like they aren't moving. They don't see any upward mobility. They want more money. They want more challenging work. The list goes on. They don't think of themselves as being bored. But what's making them miserable *is* the boredom, says Jones. That's the underlying emotion that makes them feel trapped.

If you can relate, take a breath. It's fixable. But first you need to take responsibility for your discontent. You are resourceful. Use your imagination. Do something. Make a change—even a small one.

The basic remedy for a poor attitude is to start developing a strategy to change things. When you do that, you'll feel better almost at once. The internal shift begins once you make a single step toward modifying what's getting you down. It might take some time to get what you are looking for—maybe it's a promotion—but knowing that you're taking action is energizing.

Like most things in life, with each turn, life becomes interesting again. It's the newness that piques our curiosity and sometimes scares us a little. Even if you're the only one who is aware that something's afoot and you're trying on a different behavior, it's a catalyst.

So drill down on the mental aspect of your job. Try not to waste time and energy on things that don't bear directly on your job, like office gossip, obsessing over your chief rival at work, resenting the person who always comes in late, or feeling blue because you don't have a window in your office. That's petty stuff.

Instead, surround yourself with positive coworkers. Challenge yourself to look for one new thing you can improve in your own personal work and thinking. Maybe it's smiling when you walk into the office every morning, or laughing out loud a couple of times a day. It's amazing how such things can break any tension you're feeling.

Jot down in your journal, or better yet, tell someone the funniest thing you heard or saw in the course of your working day. When you open yourself up to laughter and the humor in life, you shift a gear. It's the small changes that make the bigger change. And those have a ripple effect on your attitude about work, home, and family. They bring balance.

Create Your Own Purpose

Your attitude has a formidable effect on your behavior. You've probably heard the advice that one small positive thought in the morning can change your whole day. Try it.

Aaron Hurst, a social entrepreneur who founded the Taproot Foundation, a nonprofit aimed at encouraging professionals to do *pro bono* work, is currently CEO of Imperative, a "social benefit corporation with a mission to connect people to purpose on a massive scale." In his book, *The Purpose Economy*, he explains why America is increasingly moving toward a "purpose economy," where employees and employers make purpose a priority in their work.

People have purpose in every job and profession, he writes. "It has more to do with your attitude and approach than about the work itself," he says. Purpose is a choice. You have to stop saying your company doesn't have purpose or my job doesn't have purpose.

His mantra: You can create purpose by changing your tasks or building your relationships at work. He suggests, for instance, that by picking up the phone and actually speaking to someone or conducting an in-person meeting rather than popping someone an e-mail, you can make your work matter more to you because it is real time and adds the human touch. Tiny changes like that can have a big impact on your mind-set.

Write It Down

Earlier, I discussed journaling as a way to find what would make you love your job. Another way it's useful is in framing our outlook, which tends to be shaped by those repetitive voices in our heads: "I can't do this"; "This place stinks"; "My boss doesn't respect me."

These phrases can play like broken records, and when we're in a really bad place, they tend to be the same words over and over again. When you're feeling bad, pause and ask, "What am I thinking?" Write it down.

I can't tell you what your tape is saying, but if you write down your negative thoughts regularly, in time you will see a pattern. Once you do, then for each of those self-doubting or unenthusiastic refrains, come up with another, more positive one. If you've written down, "I can't take this anymore," then the alternative could be, "I am going to create a change."

This exercise reminds me of what used to happen when I was in grade school and a kid would get caught whispering in class. The teacher would make him go to the chalkboard and write, "I will not talk in class, I will not talk in class," 50 or so times.

There is wisdom in this method of repeating a positive phrase over and over. It becomes your default phrase, and the more likely you are to say it to yourself when you hit a roadblock. I have one I use in all kinds of situations where I feel nervous, uncomfortable, or overwhelmed, but I'm not going to share it with you. Sorry, it's personal. It's my magic; it won't be your magic. Still, I know it calms me almost instantly now that I have gone to it so many times. It helps me roll along and, yes, makes me happier. It lets me get back to concentrating on the work at hand.

So when you're on the brink of saying, "I can't take this anymore," say, "I am going to make a change." Write it down five times in your notebook; say it to yourself when you get up in the morning, whenever the spirit moves you during the day, and before you go to bed. Before you realize it, it becomes your mantra, and your attitude rallies.

A Picture Is Worth a Thousand Words

A positive image can help you pull through tough times at work, or cope with a job that's in the dumps. I call mine "going to my happy place." I close my eyes and visualize a green field in the Virginia countryside with a sweeping view of the Blue Ridge Mountains. I visualize a small hill there and atop it a blue wooden chair. I go there in my head and sit. It calms me down. I feel peaceful. My attitude shifts.

If you want a more concrete focal point than a mental image like I use, tape a picture of a special image on your office wall. Situate it someplace away from your computer and phone, so that you have to turn to look directly at it when you need to. It can be transporting. And the very action of directing your attention away from your work opens up the door in your day for a respite, a restart, and a new view. It's reviving and centering at the same time.

Build a Bear

Beverly Jones was a high-powered corporate lawyer before she changed careers to become a career coach. Back then, she came up with an image of what she called "uberBEV" to help guide her through rough patches at work.

"I envisioned an image of myself most likely to have what it would take to succeed in my job or the task at hand," she says. "I tried to identify every aspect of her . . . er . . .me—how I looked, how much I weighed, how I spoke, how much I engaged with other people. When I started to doubt myself, I would try to find just one way I could be more like uberBEV. Today, she's my friend. She's my mentor. She is about five years older than me all the time. When I don't know what to do, I try to be a little more like her."

Practice HOVERing

My acronym, HOVER, introduced in Chapter 1, stands for hope, optimism, value, enthusiasm, and resilience. It symbolizes looking down, surveying the situation, and then strategically tapping these five basic ingredients to create the change you need in your job and your life.

Hope is vital. Believe that you can reach your goals, and you will find a way to do so. My goal is for you to work on developing that crucial internal psychological muscle as you read along through this book.

Optimism involves taking an upbeat view of your work and your potential for success. For me, this is a core factor in loving what you do every day. When you're optimistic, you have a sense of enthusiasm that you can tap to take action—to see possibilities and solutions to problems at work.

This ability to have a can-do approach lets you bounce back quicker from rejection and not feel the urge to throw in the towel. It also opens your eyes to see how "you can" bring about change, not focus on how "you can't."

In my opinion, optimistic people tend to succeed in work and life because they're willing to take risks. They aren't afraid to fail because they know they will find a way to make it work and are willing to be patient and wait for it all to play out. They chip away at whatever the issue may be with the confidence that, in the end, things will improve. And with each little chip, things will improve.

One way to develop optimism is to focus on what's going right and stop thinking so much about what is going wrong—or could. Again, I find that keeping a journal can help with this. If you notice that the same concerns, worries, and pessimistic views keep cropping up, it will help you see that you need to either make some changes or let it go. And always keep a "good" list, or a gratitude list, as some people call it. Use your list to reset your day, every day. Be grateful.

Optimism flows from gratitude. Thankfulness is a great antidote to what ails you. Routinely take note of the things you like the most about your job. Give yourself a moment or two to be grateful for whatever those things are. Reach out and thank someone who does a good turn for you or made your work shine in some way. It makes you both feel good. An e-mail is fine, but a handwritten note is always classy. The trick is to physically feel the gratitude in your heart. It might be something as straightforward as laughing with a colleague who works in the cubicle next to you, or appreciating the nuances of the architecture of the buildings you pass on your walk to the office.

This isn't just platitude time. Mean it, and take this exercise seriously. I try to think of at least one work-related thing I am grateful for each day. For me, it can be as simple as interacting with a colleague in a LinkedIn group, or tweeting about a story written by a respected journalist I follow that I think others will benefit from reading. Then maybe that writer will notice that I liked his story by favoriting it or retweeting to his followers what I had to say about it. I feel great when someone I respect retweets one of my online articles, too.

And so it goes. Interactions with others, even virtual ones, can get you unstuck and make you feel that someone notices you and your work. You feel valued.

There are days when I'm dazed with deadlines and I'm uneasy with the pressure. But when I pause and remember these good moments, those negative feelings dissipate. It's a dose of mental relief and an opportunity to push the restart button.

Value is critical. This means having the inner confidence to know that if you put out the effort, you will get results or see progress. It means *you* yourself value your own work and skills and talents. It means you believe in yourself. That inner compass, pulled by confidence, will help direct your actions. It's subtle, but those around you will sense and respond to it.

One way to build your sense of value is to continually be learning new things. To deal effectively with making changes in your work life, it helps to be engaged in changing yourself. The most inventive people I know frequently get involved in learning or self-improvement efforts. It's fun. When you do so, everything else around you becomes more interesting. When you're acquiring knowledge, you notice the world around you. You spot things. You listen better. Your mind turns on.

So if you can just do one thing to make a change right now, learn something new. If you can't make it work related, do it in the context of your life. Take a course in glassblowing or an acting class. Go on a learning vacation—a cooking school in Ireland or a wooden boat–building course in Maine. Sign up for a series of lectures at your local community center or library. Something as simple as participating in a monthly book club can get your mind engaged.

Maggie Mistal, one of my go-to career coaches, for example, attended a jewelry-making course at Harmony Hill Farm located in South Coventry, Pennsylvania. "Though I don't think I'll make a career out of that talent," she says, "the course was so much more than that. It was exactly the boost of inspiration I needed as well as a fun, easy place to let my hair down and refocus on the priorities most important in my life and work."

If you persistently add worth to what you bring to the job and to your life, chances are your manager or boss will take note and reward you for it. When we feel valued both from inside ourselves and from others, we give back to others and perhaps ultimately to our employer. Everyone gains.

Enthusiasm is the intangible get-up-and-go factor that boosts your energy and helps you tackle changes both internal and external. When you're enthusiastic, people want what you have. They want to be around you. They want you to be on their team. Enthusiasm is infectious, and it's invigorating.

Bottom line: Being eager to try new things and see the upside of a project can lead you to interesting assignments and opportunities that will bring happiness to your work life in ways you may never have envisioned.

Resilience, or a knack for springing back in the face of adversity or failure, is imperative in achieving happiness at work. When you are resilient, you are attuned to spotting trends and turning them into opportunities. Resilient people resist the urge to get bogged down in the past, and instead keep looking toward the future. They're curious. They keep learning.

You can teach yourself to be resilient. You can learn to be more comfortable in an environment where nothing stays the same and the old ways may no longer work. When you gain resilience, you can create a more successful career path, and at the same time find greater enjoyment in the rest of your life.

So get your HOVER on. If you want to love your job, you will need to find ways to incorporate these qualities in your tool kit. Not everyone can put together all these pieces at the same time, of course, but it's what you're striving toward.

BEV'S SIX THINGS YOU CAN DO TO BUILD RESILIENCE

I asked career coach Beverly Jones for her insights on how to build career resilience for my Forbes.com "Second Verse" column. She built on some of the concepts I alluded to earlier. Here's what she said:

As an executive coach, I know that the path to professional success isn't what it used to be. When we Baby Boomers entered the job market, career success could be a matter of climbing onto the right organizational ladder, and then hanging on. As a young lawyer I was pretty much told, "Be loyal to the company and the company will be loyal to you."

Today, the idea of spending your entire career in a single organization, keeping your head down and doing pretty much the same type of work, seems quaint. Your career can be expected to flow through many phases, encompassing numerous organizations, shifting skills sets, and startling change.

I've worked with hundreds of leaders and high-achieving professionals, and I've learned that you can't predict where your career path will take you. But you can prepare for it. Once, a central characteristic for success was loyalty. Today, what you need is resilience.

(continued)

Resilience brings security in a constantly changing world. Resilience means anticipating risks and feeling comfortable with change. Resilience involves limiting damage during turbulent times, absorbing hard knocks, regrouping, and bouncing back when the worst happens. It's the ability to start feeling better and bolster your confidence after a setback. It's remaining engaged in the midst of shifting challenges. Whether you're a college student wondering about your first real job, or a Boomer thinking about alternatives to retirement, resilience means being able to evolve with the times.

You *can* build resilience. Resilient people aren't necessarily born with a unique ability to bounce back or forge ahead. Rather, they are ordinary folks who learn behaviors, attitudes, and work patterns that allow them to keep going and growing, even in difficult or uncertain times.

Here are six tips for building resilience:

1. *Get connected.* Develop a strong network of positive relationships. Don't wait until there's a crisis; start now to methodically extend your circle. Go out to events even when you don't feel like it. Join groups. Recruit mentors and find ways to mentor others. Look for ways to support friends, colleagues, and even casual business acquaintances. And know that they will be there to accept, support, and inspire you during the hard times.

2. *Choose optimism.* Positive people are more resilient than pessimists, and you can work to become more optimistic. A starting point is to stop thinking so much about what goes wrong and start focusing on what goes right. Keeping a journal can help you do that. If you notice that the same old worries and regrets keep going through your mind, write those thoughts down and decide whether you want to let them go or address them in some way. And start keeping a record of the good things. At the end of each day, write a few lines about what went well and what you're most grateful for in your current situation.

3. *Learn something new.* To deal effectively with change, it helps to be engaged in changing yourself. The most innovative and resilient professionals tend to frequently engage in learning or improvement efforts. When you're in the process of learning, your viewpoint changes, and you spot connections that you never noticed before. If you don't know what to do next, start learning something new.

4. *Think like an entrepreneur.* Know that you own your career and that nobody else is going to chart your path. Even if you feel like a cog in the middle of a big organizational wheel, you can run your career like a one-person business. And that will help ease your transition if you need to make one. Think about your brand, recognize who your customers and bosses are, and be clear about what they pay you for. Look for new ways to add value, in effect expanding your range of product offerings.

5. *Look at the big picture.* Let go of your preoccupation with this week and think about how success might look for you five years from now. And know that your career can't soar when you're neglecting the rest of your life. Write a brief personal vision statement, make a list, or draw a diagram touching on your most important values and the key parts of your life. Even when you're engaged in a career crisis, you will feel better if you can keep your perspective.

6. *Get in shape.* Your career is influenced by everything you do to stay in shape—physically, emotionally, and spiritually. To do your best work, and to build the resilience that will keep you going, manage your fitness and energy level, as well as your time.

Mental Games

At the end of your workday, spend a minute thinking about the three longest interactions with other people you had that day, advises Barbara L. Fredrickson, a pioneer scientist in positive psychology at the University of North Carolina at Chapel Hill. It might be face to face, by phone, or by e-mail, but it should be a bona fide conversational connection.

Ask yourself how close emotionally you feel to the people you were interacting with. You'll get a subtle cue reminding you that each time you connect with someone else at work is an opportunity for something more than just an exchange of goods or information. It's the human touch. We feed off of each other's emotions and, well, humanity. We learn to empathize. When you learn to cultivate these each day, it's easier to let negativity roll by.

Also ask yourself how many times each day you saddle yourself with needless negativity. Turn off the negative loop running through your head. Instead, ask yourself: "What is going right for me? What can I be thankful for?"

Self-acceptance is the foundation for positivity. Lightening up on ourselves allows us to get more joy out of what we do. We can spend all our time focusing on what's going wrong; problems grab our attention and pull us down that proverbial negative rabbit hole. But we can also say, "Okay, the problems are here, but what's going well?" Asking yourself that question can be a powerful way to change your inner chatter to let you feel more open, more alive, and more likely to connect with others.

Step outside of your own head and focus on the good things that are happening to other people, suggests Fredrickson. It's the "it's five o'clock somewhere" approach. If you don't have something good going on in your life, celebrate someone else's good fortune. Recognize it as a source of your joy, rather than resentment. It is not a zero-sum game.

Finally, to reiterate what Jones suggests, when you think like an entrepreneur, you're also happier. You picture yourself in control, driving your career. The key is training your psyche to act as if you're always running your own small business—and your major client, so to speak—is your employer. Says Leonard J. Glick, professor of management and organizational development at Northeastern University, who teaches the art of motivating employees for a living, "It contributes to a feeling of 'it's mine,' and most people, when it's theirs, don't want to fail, don't want poor-quality work."

Entrepreneurial thinking has a domino effect. Your work improves, and so does your sense of pride in what you are doing.

Adjusting Your Attitude

Here are some action steps you can take to improve your internal motivation right now:

1. *Focus on the people around you.* My 16-year-old niece and I recently stood in the customs border-control line in Philadelphia when returning from a trip to Paris. The line was long, and everyone was tired from the nearly nine-hour flight. We were all cranky and eager to get to the other side.

   The customs agent in the booth was an older gentleman, and our line was moving slowly. I had no doubt he had been doing this job for years. He was in no hurry. With each person who stepped up with his or her passport, he smiled and struck up a pleasant conversation, meeting their eyes. Each one seemed to brighten when he spoke to them.

   My niece and I were shifting from foot to foot, anxious for the line to move faster. But then it dawned on me—this guy really loved his job. Other agents down the line appeared stern and perfunctory, slamming down their stamp and barking "next." They looked glum.

   But not our agent. Yes, he was sitting in a tiny booth, performing the routine task of stamping passports and facing weary people eager to get past him. Yet he seemed to be having a good time. It was infectious.

   I commented on this to my niece, and I suddenly relaxed. She started watching him with a different eye and laughed out loud. When we finally reached his booth, he asked me what I did for a living. When I said I was a writer, he asked me who my favorite author was, told me that his was Somerset Maugham, and asked if I had taken my niece to the well-known Ernest Hemingway haunts in Paris—Les Deux Magots and Closerie des Lilas. I smiled and said I had. He smiled. A human win all around in my book. And I honestly believe he loves his job. He made a difference in our day, too.

2. *Change it up.* Making simple changes to your work schedule can be a boost. If you're an early riser, plan a morning walk before you head to the office. Or make an effort to have

lunch with someone new once a week or even every other week. It doesn't have to be someone from your office.

3. *Surround yourself with positive people.* Look for chances to be with doers. You'll feel more inspired if your life includes people who are out there taking part in interesting activities, traveling, pursuing hobbies, and generally enjoying life.

4. *Be mindful.* Slow down. Do one thing at a time, with focus. This is pretty simple advice. But when you tune out all the distractions and stop multitasking, you can pay full attention to what you're doing. You concentrate. You calm down. For me, it's something as basic as clicking the ringer off my phone while I am writing an article.

What to Do If You're Bullied at Work

An all-too-common reason for feeling miserable at work is bullying. It isn't just about school kids or athletes. It's rampant in many workplaces, no matter the industry, and it can make your job hell. I'm not suggesting bullying is something you personally can change from within, but it falls into the category of things that can make you feel bad inside and can have everything to do with whether or not you love to go to work.

One-third of people surveyed say they've been bullied on the job, according to the Bellingham, Washington–based Workplace Bullying Institute. Half of the organizations surveyed by the Society for Human Resource Management (SHRM) reported incidents of bullying in their workplaces. And it's not usually coming from that proverbial bad boss whom we all like to gripe about: 82 percent of workplace bullying incidents took place among peers.

Bullying can take many shapes and forms. It might be verbal abuse from a coworker, such as swearing and intimidation, snide comments, or unrelenting teasing. It could be someone taking credit for your work or trying to make you look incompetent. If it is the boss who's the problem, bullying can mean shouting, constant criticism, the creation of impossible expectations, and the shifting of expectations at the last minute to set you up to fail.

And, yes, bullying occurs through technology, such as Facebook and other social media. This kind accounted for about one in five incidents, the SHRM survey found.

It may surprise you to learn that workplace bullying isn't always illegal (although legislation has been proposed in 25 states), unless it's based on age, race, disability, gender, or religion. Speaking up can be complicated. Whom do you talk to—the bully, the boss, or the people in human resources (HR)? What are the possible repercussions of speaking up?

Here are five moves you can make to handle a tough situation at work.

1. *Size up the situation.* Do some soul-searching to be sure that your side of the street is clean. Is your work truly top-drawer? Is your attitude positive? Being able to answer yes will be a huge help if you go public with a complaint.

   Be certain that you're not being too thin-skinned about things that you probably should let roll off your back.

   Another question to consider is whether anyone else is getting the same rough treatment.

   If you need to vent or get advice, be discreet and talk to someone not connected to your workplace. You don't want to be the one feeding the rumor mill.

   "Choose your moments carefully," says George Schofield, a career expert and psychologist. "Decide when you need to stand up for yourself and when it simply isn't worth it." (Not reporting, it turns out, is a common decision: About 43 percent of bullying victims said they didn't report their bullying to anyone in the organization, the SHRM survey found.)

2. *Document it.* Write down what's happening—dates, times, and locations. This journal should detail specific volatile behavior and give an explanation of what started it and your recommendations for how it would be better handled next time, says Schofield: "A grievance list alone won't be enough." Keep your log stored in a safe place such as a home computer rather than a work computer.

3. *Talk to the bully.* Have a one-on-one talk with the bully—but only if you truly feel confident and physically secure. Be positive and do your best to be polite. Calmly explain that it's not

okay to treat you this way. It's possible the person is unaware that what he or she is doing is upsetting you and will apologize and back off. You'll need some backbone here. But it's not in your job description to accept rude behavior or irrational work demands.

4. *Take your complaint to a higher power.* Bullies can be tenacious and unreasonable, so you may need to call in the big guns. Your first line of defense is to talk to your immediate supervisor, assuming he or she is not the culprit. But you may have to go to HR.

   Many employers are well aware that workplace bullying can put a damper on morale and increase employee turnover. Both repercussions can increase costs and nick profits— and no organization likes to see that happen. So it's little wonder that though bullying isn't illegal, the SHRM survey found that 43 percent of employers had some kind of policy against it, and 13 percent were planning to institute one. It's usually tucked into an employee handbook or code of conduct. Many workplaces have mandatory classes that teach employees how to recognize harassment. Employers typically respond to provable bullying allegations with actions like reassignment or obligatory anger management training. Suspension or firing is a last resort.

   If you take your complaint to your boss or HR, frame it constructively; don't whine. Yes, it's an emotional grievance. But you must make an objective case about the cost of bullying to the organization. Appeal to bottom-line issues—turnover, absenteeism, and litigation. Have your documentation pulled together. Describe every incident in precise detail, including dates and times, and explain how the situation is taking a toll on your ability to do your work.

   "Avoid locking yourself into the good guy versus bad guy trap," says Schofield. "Remember that there are always multiple viewpoints. Focus on the potential solution more than the existing problem."

   If you've concluded that after you hit age 40 you're being bullied, harassed by a boss or coworkers, or if you notice that other older workers are also targeted, and you believe the harassment is based on age, you should report it to your employer's HR department right away, says Donna Ballman, an employment lawyer and author *of Stand Up for Yourself Without Getting Fired: Resolve Workplace Issues Before You Quit, Get Axed, or Sue the Bastards.*

You should call your filing a "Formal Complaint of Age-Based Harassment." It should lay out how you (and other older employees, if any) are being targeted for treatment different than younger employees, Ballman says. Ask the employer to take prompt action to correct the situation. If no corrective action is taken, or if you are retaliated against, it may be time to talk to an employment lawyer or the U.S. Equal Employment Opportunity Commission (EEOC). Complaints about age discrimination are protected by law against retaliation. You can read more on age discrimination at eeoc.gov. Be aware that there are time limitations for bringing claims to the EEOC.

Complaints about discrimination based on race, sex, national origin, disability, religion, or other statuses are also protected against retaliation. But if you're not being bullied for any of these reasons, Ballman suggests that you find other employees who are also being bullied for other reasons and complain on behalf of them and yourself. In those other cases, she says, "While complaining alone and just for yourself may not be protected against retaliation, once you act on behalf of others, you may have legal protection."

If your employer retaliates against you for complaining, and you're a nonsupervisory worker at a private company, you can report the conduct to the National Labor Relations Board.

5. *Come up with Plan B sooner rather than later.* The unpleasant truth is that many employees who get caught in a bullying scenario wind up moving to another department within the organization or leaving altogether. "You don't have to change jobs or employers soon, but waiting to create Plan B until you're out of time is a very weak approach," Schofield says.

Don't spread the word at your workplace that you're looking, but go ahead and update your resume. Strengthen your job marketability by updating or expanding your skills. Check out the Plus 50 Initiative by the American Association of Community Colleges aimed at students over 50. Most colleges and universities offer distance and adult education programs as well, and there's been an explosion of online education programs such as Coursera.

And there's no time like the present to subtly tap your professional network. Reconnect with old friends and colleagues through lunch, coffee, or social media such as LinkedIn and Facebook. Attend industry and alumni networking functions. At this stage, you're not asking the people you meet for help landing a job. But you never know where you might hear of that lead that just might spring you from your current situation.

Step Right Up and Enroll in My Three-Step Fitness Program

Feeling fit improves your sense of well-being in all aspects of your life and lays the groundwork for the work you need to do to fall in love with your job again. This ultimate fitness trio creates a feeling of nimbleness and allows you to make good choices in your work life.

Part I: Get in Shape Financially

Having trouble focusing on your job? Productivity lagging? Calling in sick? Blame it on your bills.

HR managers say many employees are so freaked out about their finances that it's hurting their job performance, according to a survey by the SHRM.

I get it. If you've ever had night sweats about paying your bills, you probably get it, too. But who'd have thought Big Brother was watching?

Your boss is on to you. The majority of the HR professionals canvassed in the survey said their employees were grappling with more personal financial challenges than they were five years ago. And a whopping 83 percent said those challenges have an obvious impact on overall employee performance. The top performance problems:

- Ability to focus on work (47 percent).
- Overall employee stress (46 percent).

- Overall employee productivity (26 percent).
- Absent or late to work (24 percent).
- Health problems (12 percent).

Employees' most common money worries? Almost half of HR professionals said an "overall lack of monetary funds to cover their personal expenses" was the biggest challenge employees face, followed by medical expenses, retirement savings, credit card debt, and home mortgage payments.

Not surprisingly, professionals at organizations whose employees were primarily Baby Boomers said their workers were mostly worried they weren't saving enough for retirement, while those at companies with younger workers said the main culprit was high credit card debt.

The financial pressure is draining retirement accounts, too. Almost three-quarters of HR professionals said their employees were more likely to dip into employer-sponsored retirement savings plans in the past 12 months compared with previous years.

And many workers weren't saving enough or saving at all.

But if workers recognize they need to save more to ensure a comfortable retirement, why aren't they doing so? More than half say they simply can't afford it due to the cost of living and the press of day-to-day expenses, according to the 2014 Retirement Confidence Survey conducted by the nonpartisan Employee Benefit Research Institute. Other reasons for not saving, or not saving more, for retirement include these:

- Currently unemployed or underemployed (14 percent).
- Paying off nonmortgage debt (6 percent).
- Paying off a mortgage or housing expenses (5 percent).
- Education expenses (5 percent).

Fifty-eight percent of workers report having a problem with their level of debt. And almost a quarter say their current level of debt is higher than it was five years ago.

This, of course, begs the question. Are employers doing anything to help employees get it together? Big firms, those with 2,500 to 24,999 employees, are more apt to provide financial education of some type than are small businesses with fewer than 100 workers. What's stopping them? Roughly a quarter of HR professionals said that the cost of providing financial education and lack of interest among employees are the biggest obstacles holding them back.

What? Free financial advice and guidance is a lifeline that I'm amazed anyone would snub. But I suppose it's possible.

The companies that do offer employees a hand use an array of methods. Most provide an employee assistance program that includes some financial planning counseling. Others offer education on budgeting, ways to pay for education, debt reduction, credit card use, homeownership, and taxes, according to the survey. That's a good thing. So if you're having trouble, look into your employer's benefits.

Many firms, however, limit the education to helping you figure out how to use your employer-provided benefits, such as 401(k) plans, health insurance, and flexible spending accounts. Not as good, but take what you can get.

Even if your company does provide help, you might still be in the dark. Employers typically trot out financial education through "voluntary seminars during work hours using outside speakers," according to the survey. But who the heck is going to cut into their on-the-job productivity, or their one free lunch hour, by stopping in on a voluntary seminar during the workday?

It's possible you were told about your company's financial education initiative during your new-hire employee orientation. Your firm's intranet, too, may also have material. But seriously, who taps into their employer's web site to learn about saving money when they have time to float around online? Did someone say "Facebook"?

The upshot of the survey: The employer-employee financial stress breakdown is worrisome for both parties. For me, it's clear. You can't skip financial literacy. And while it would be dandy if your employer would offer a helping hand, unless a law is passed that requires them to do so, the final responsibility is yours alone.

It works like dominos. The less you know about your finances and investing, the less you save, and the lower your chances of living within your means and socking enough away for a retirement. If you're feeling anxious about your finances, don't moon around the office and call in sick. Do something about it.

- Take an evening class in personal finance at a community college.
- Tap into free planning and investor education centers on no-load mutual fund web sites like Fidelity.com, Troweprice.com, and Vanguard.com.
- Track your finances on sites like Mint.com and Youneedabudget. com. These free sites are designed to help you streamline your bill paying and dissect your monthly spending. For help with your student loans, go to Finovera, MoneyStream, and Tuition.io.
- Check out the National Endowment for Financial Education's site, Smartaboutmoney.org, which offers a library with free guides that explain stocks, bonds, and mutual funds. Morningstar, the investment and mutual fund advisory firm, has two parts on its site aimed at novices: Investing Classroom and Start Investing. And the government site, Investor.gov, is worth a look as well. Go to the U.S. Treasury web site www.mymoney. gov, an independent educational resource.
- Find a fee-only financial planner. Look for experienced, credentialed advisers. As a rule, I think an adviser should have the Certified Financial Planner designation, awarded by the nonprofit Certified Financial Planner Board of Standards. These national groups of financial planners offer searchable databases with contact information: the Certified Financial Planner Board of Standards (CFP.net), Financial Planning Association (Plannersearch.org), Garrett Planning Network (garrettplanningnetwork.com), and National Association of Personal Financial Advisors (NAPFA.org).

If your employer doesn't offer financial planning and retirement seminars, ask your HR department if it would do so if enough employees were interested.

Don't risk losing a good job or a promotion because you're so stressed out about finances. Put on your poker face. HR is watching.

Remember, too, that if you are following my advice about life-long learning and adding new skills, doing so can come with a financial price tag. It might mean a tuition bill to upgrade your skills. It could be a reduction in pay if you move to a new position with your employer that has more purpose but pays less or offers fewer hours. That makes being financially fit that much more important. Financial fitness gives you the freedom to make choices. You are not trapped and held ransom by your paycheck.

Here are some ways to get your money life together:

- *Chart a budget.* Write down your income, what you owe, and what you have socked away. Look at what you're spending every day, every month, and every year. This will help you find ways to pare back your spending. Begin by writing down in a notebook exactly what you spend each day. Then, on a monthly basis, study your credit card and bank statements to see where your money is going and what can be trimmed back or eliminated. Do you dine out too often? Are you traveling too much? Do you send your clothes to the dry cleaners too frequently? You can save on the gasoline tab for your car by taking public transportation more frequently. How about finding a group to car pool with to work? Or riding your bike to work and getting some exercise while you're at it?
- *Put money away in an emergency fund.* A savings cushion of six months to a year of living expenses to cover unexpected crises will stave off dipping into your retirement savings or taking on debt.
- *Review your credit report and score.* Many employers are now checking them prior to promoting their employees or even transitioning them to a new department at work. They must ask your permission to do so, however. Check for errors by obtaining a free annual report at annualcreditreport.com.

  If your credit score is low, improve it. Best moves: "Always pay your bills on time," says Gerri Detweiler, the credit expert at Credit.com. "One late payment can hit your score hard." Don't open new accounts, transfer balances, or shut down accounts if you know an employer might ask to see your report.
- *Eliminate debt.* Talk about a stress buster. This process can take some time, but tackle those credit card bills and refinance your mortgage at a lower rate, if possible. Consider downsizing your home, depending on where you live and the real

estate market. You might be able to move to a smaller home and even pay cash from the proceeds of your new digs from the proceeds from the home you sold, or at least take on a smaller mortgage. Check out advice from the ever-resourceful Jeff Yeager at his The Ultimate Cheapskate web site. His mantra: "Spend less, enjoy life more."

Part II: Get Physically Fit

You don't have to run a super-fast mile or bench-press your weight, I always say, but you do need to be in decent physical shape. Fitness gives you the strength and mental acuity to cope with stress, particularly when making any workplace decisions.

It sounds shallow, but a fit and robust appearance is an advantage in the work world. Employers notice that spark of vitality and positivity. It subtly says you're up for the job and for taking on new challenges. And you feel better about yourself, too. It is an attitude pick-me-up that is good for you in many ways.

Develop a workout routine that you can stick to. You might have to ramp up slowly, but it will have a lasting impact on your life. There are plenty of options out there.

I walk. Start with at least a half hour, say, three or four times a week. You can build from there. My Labrador retriever keeps me accountable for much of this activity. She demands at least four miles a few times a week and shorter distances on other days.

Working with a personal trainer at a local fitness club or taking classes will keep you accountable for showing up. You might also enroll in a yoga class, Tai Chi, or qigong. There is a wide variety of yoga formats, for instance, some more aggressive than others. If you like to swim, seek out a Y or a local high school with a swimming pool.

A healthy diet is part of your fitness regime, too. Nutritious eating will lift your energy level and bring a healthy glow to your skin and hair. Drink lots of water, eat fruits and vegetables, and go light on the red meat.

It's important to set some goals for how much exercise you desire or how many pounds you'd like to lose to feel happier and healthier. Regular sleeping patterns are also *de rigeur* in building your healthy lifestyle.

Part III: Seek Spiritual Fitness

I firmly believe that anyone going through a job shift must find a quiet space internally that offers respite from the stress and anxieties that go along with making and asking for changes in our lives. One way is meditation and mindfulness. It can improve your brain's focus and awareness and your general state of health.

Studies show that meditation can slow your heart rate and normalize your blood pressure. Advocates say it can rally your immune system and help you generate fewer stress hormones like adrenaline and cortisol. Moreover, like exercise, it often incites the brain to discharge neurotransmitters such as dopamine, serotonin, and endorphins that increase inner feelings of happiness.

In my experience, mind-body balance allows you to coolly weather the thumps in life and teaches you to tranquilly heed the inner voice that can guide your choices. Joining a meditation group is one way to get started.

You might also consider learning ikebana, the Japanese art of flower arrangement. It is more than simply putting flowers in a container. The practice embodies a spiritual aspect. I have several friends, women and men, who are deeply committed to this art form and regularly take classes to advance their skills. They tell me it helps them live in the moment. Silence is a requirement during the practice.

For me, walking gets me to that place. I can close my eyes as I move down a country road and lose myself in the rhythm of my steps and the sounds of the gravel. There are other ways to find a pace to escape your own chattering brain. Volunteering can help you see your own trials with new eyes. I have found that it provides the karma to push onward toward your new goals with a sense of calm and purpose. Find your own way to reach that quiet space.

In essence, my three-pronged fitness program delivers:

- Release from debt, which can give you the freedom to take a chance on trying something new.
- The enthusiasm and energy and optimism that come from physical fitness.
- The calm, stress-free inner balance that having spiritual fitness produces.

Chapter Recap

In this chapter, you looked inward to find ways to make small changes to your attitude and improve your mental game. By hitting the refresh button, you ramped up your energy and began to explore ways to take your work to another level starting from the inside out. You discovered that it's not always about you. When you're happy for other people, it makes you feel good. When you say thanks, you feel good. We are all in this together, after all.

You stretched to have more meaningful connections with coworkers. You began to pause to reflect on the positive aspects of your day before you headed home for the night.

You learned about the overarching concept of HOVER—hope, optimism, value, enthusiasm, and resilience—and why tapping into these simple feelings lets you reframe your way of thinking about work. Meanwhile, by pushing yourself to practice getting in touch with these core positive feelings on a daily basis, you began to build those muscles and grow stronger emotionally. And, importantly, you discovered my three-part fitness program—physical, financial, and spiritual—the trio of essential non-work-related tools that will help you find solutions to your workplace blues.

Your To-Do List

- Start developing a strategy to change things and improve your attitude one step at a time.
- Laugh more.
- Spend 20 minutes writing in your journal about what your "purpose" in your work is right now.
- When you're feeling bad, ask yourself, "What am I thinking?" and write it down.
- Create a positive image of yourself, and write that down.
- Practice HOVERing.
- If you are being bullied at work, figure out ways to fix the situation.
- Start a fitness program to get in shape physically, financially, and spiritually.

Beyond the Job Description

■ ■ ■

Roberta Terkowitz, a former business development specialist for IBM's cloud computing unit in the Washington, D.C., area, insisted that it was the work around the borders of her job that had been a big factor in keeping her work life happy.

"I found ways to nibble at the edge and add little bits to my work day that were even more fulfilling than the actual work at times," says the 30-year information technology (IT) veteran. Terkowitz discovered ways to get excited about her work by looking beyond the official parameters of her job.

She is now recently retired from IBM, but I found her approach instructive. I'll get to the myriad of ways she did this in a minute. The lesson, as you will see from her story, is that you can do things on the edges of your job that can give it meaning and make it fun and challenging again—or for the first time.

In this chapter, we will explore ways you can push yourself to try new things and different approaches to your work. Not all of them will be options for you. My suggestions are meant to get you thinking about what *is* possible if you push yourself to look beyond the confines of your job per se, to pull your eyes up from your cell phone and away from your computer, and really look around to see what might be out there for you.

Perhaps you could get involved in an industry association or ask to take on a special project or assume new duties. You could be a volunteer or a mentor or seek out a new mentor for yourself. You could nurture relationships with coworkers and meet new people in your office. You could even find ways to improve your working relationships, including those with a younger boss, which would ease your workplace tension or malaise.

"You are only limited by your own imagination," my late father always used to say to me, and I live his advice to this day. It's entirely up to you to motivate yourself. Don't expect anyone to do it for you. We're all accountable for our own actions.

Take Time for Renewal

Terkowitz began by raising her hand to be the chair of the Strategic Forecast Council and Federal IT Day for the TechAmerica Foundation, an industry association. "That was my way of giving back to the industry that I'd worked in for so many years," she told me.

In addition to her association work, she volunteered to brief foreign delegations that visit the IBM Institute for Electronic Government on new technology. Mentoring coworkers was another part of her mojo. "I enjoyed helping others succeed, particularly when they were new to a job," Terkowitz says. "All of these efforts added a spice to my work world that otherwise wouldn't have been there."

But there's more to it. Terkowitz also took concrete steps to revitalize her own career within IBM. While she had found success in her mostly sales- and marketing-oriented positions, in many ways the work itself had grown stale. But before she could make a move, her world shifted. She was diagnosed with breast cancer in 2006. "It makes you realize there's no such thing as 'someday.' If you are not enjoying yourself today, change something because 'someday' may not come around," she says.

And she did. Once she was cancer free, she applied for and was selected to be one of the first 100 participants in IBM's Corporate Service Corps, a sort of corporate version of the Peace Corps that combines global leadership development with skilled assistance to developing countries. (See "IBM Corporate Service Corps at Work.")

IBM CORPORATE SERVICE CORPS AT WORK

IBM's Corporate Service Corps focuses on building its employees' skills, from leadership to teamwork to technical knowhow. The firm sends employees like Roberta Terkowitz to help local governments, small businesses, and nonprofits in the developing world. "We don't view it as traditional charity work because employees go to places where we have an interest in building IBM's visibility and where we need to better understand the cultural, political, technology, and business landscapes," says Ari Fishkind, IBM media relations manager, Corporate Citizenship and Corporate Affairs. "The experts we send are highly skilled, although we often have them 'stretch' by performing technical work outside their comfort zone. We don't just send techies; we send experts in law, finance, marketing, business, and human resources."

IBM has found that this is a more effective—and cost-efficient—way to build talent, he says. Traditionally, the company would send "a lucky few senior executives (and their families) abroad at great expense to an already-developed market," Fishkind explained to me. "They would spend a long time there—probably only sticking to the company of fellow expats—and we'd also have to backfill their position. They may or may not have come back with super-valuable insights."

Some 3,000 IBM participants from 58 countries have participated in more than 1,000 CSC projects in 37 countries, generating more than $100 million in value for host organizations over a six-year period. According to a 2013 IBM-administered survey of Corporate Service Corps alumni, the Corps is helping IBM employees develop leadership and problem-solving skills. Nine out of 10 employees who participated thought that this was one of the best leadership development experiences that IBM offers. Eight out of 10 thought that it increased their desire to complete their careers at IBM. Nine out of 10 managers would recommend that other employees apply for the program, and 8 out

(continued)

of 10 managers thought it improved their employees' motivation.

It's not just a feel-good experience for the employees; the work also has a lasting impact. For instance, the Corps helped Nigeria design a program to provide financial, health care, and literacy assistance to poor women and children. In Senegal, IBM worked with Coders4Africa to provide African computer coders with business training to complement their technical skills. As a result, three proposed software projects have received funding to build key mobile and cloud solutions in health care, agriculture, and field data collection. In Vietnam, a team helped a key travel agency increase its business while aiding the country's economic development. In Brazil, IBM's advice enabled a network of dozens of children's hospitals and youth centers to become more efficient.

Terkowitz's team of eight lived in a local guesthouse in Tanzania for a month, where she worked for the African Wildlife Foundation on a project to bring ecotourism and its revenue to villagers in Wildlife Management Areas of the Maasai Steppe. She came back from the experience emboldened to leave her professional comfort zone. She asked to be transferred to a different part of the IBM business—Cloud Business Development. Her goal: to learn and apply the organizational and improvisational skills she honed in Africa in a less hierarchical area of IBM.

The Cloud group actually resembled something of a start-up, said Terkowitz. Plus, there were no sales goals to meet, no one reporting to her. "It wasn't like I made a big change, and I didn't make it right away. What I realized, though, is, 'My gosh, I could do so much more than I ever thought I could do.'"

I love Terkowitz's proactive approach to falling in love with her work.

Another IBM employee, Sharon Dinneen, a project manager for the department run by IBM's chief information officer, has worked for IBM since 1996. While her office is in Cambridge, Massachusetts, she works mostly from her home in Dunstable, Massachusetts, about 39 miles from Boston.

In the last five years, she has been assigned to two-week stints in China, Germany, and Ireland, and, most recently, was a member of an IBM Corporate Service Corps team that spent time in Izmir, Turkey. Team members hailed from the United Kingdom, Ireland, Mexico, the United States, India, Australia, and Malaysia.

While Dinneen is a part of a worldwide team at IBM, most of her interactions with co-workers are via telephone. So the chance to get out of her home office and tackle a different dynamic working with people face to face has been "personally and professionally fulfilling," she says. "It has encouraged me to take risks, improvise, go outside of my comfort zone, and stretch my skills." Another bonus: She finds that as a result of her experiences, she is a "smarter listener."

You too must take similar steps to get out of your rut. In *Create Your Future the Peter Drucker Way*, author Bruce Rosenstein writes about ways to build your future beyond your current workplace based on management guru Drucker's principles. Drucker believed, as Rosenstein writes, "If you are not satisfied with where things are now, do something about it. If the idea of a legacy spurs you to action, that's fine, but I think it also means accepting the need for renewal and becoming a different person."

This is clearly your time to accept "the need for renewal" and take action, or you wouldn't be reading this book. As Rosenstein explains, Drucker said that individuals should think beyond a career to ask questions of themselves, Rosenstein explains: "Who am I? What do I want to be? What do I want to put into life? What do I want to get out of it?" These are very basic and broad, but take them seriously. Spend some time formulating your answers, and write them down in your journal.

Volunteering and Mentoring

Drucker also wrote about what Rosenstein characterizes as "the need to have genuine interests beyond your main work." He felt that "everyone must keep growing and developing, gaining intellectual stimulation as a way of guarding against the inevitable disappointments that come with any job."

I couldn't agree more. Drucker nailed it with the concept that by participating in a range of activities beyond your career, energy will flow back into all aspects of your life, including your work.

Volunteering, mentoring, and sponsoring are some smart ways to get the ball rolling. Here are some tips to get started.

Do Volunteer Work

Look for opportunities to volunteer for a nonprofit organization. Volunteering gets you outside of your own head and that swamp of negativity and helps you gain some perspective on others' needs. When it's a volunteer effort that's initiated by your employer, it builds relationships with coworkers, and perhaps even your boss, as you work side by side to make a difference outside of the office hierarchy. An esprit de corps emerges.

Check with your human resources (HR) department or supervisor to see what volunteer projects may already be in place and see how you can get involved. Many corporations are well aware of the value of touting their good works and have built social-purpose projects into their corporate culture. It's a dual-pronged approach that allows them to be good corporate citizens while also keeping their employees engaged.

To respond to the tragic events of September 11, 2001, every year on that date AARP sets aside a Day of Service, where employees volunteer to give back to their communities via hundreds of projects. Across the country, for instance, AARP staff members have worked together to pack food at the Regional Food Bank of Oklahoma in Oklahoma City or the Valley View Community Food Bank in Sun City, Arizona. They have beautified a peace garden in Baltimore in honor of those who lost their lives on September 11. They have helped build flower boxes and paint at an elementary school, and around Washington, D.C., picked up trash from the Theodore Roosevelt Island trails.

In a recent General Electric report, one thing that stood out was the question of retention, according to Raghu Krishnamoorthy, GE's vice president of executive development and chief learning officer. "The feedback from the firm's employees was: Don't try to retain us; instead, inspire us to stay," he wrote in a recent blog for *Forbes*.

As a result, GE's many businesses try to embed a sense of mission for their employees. One way that GE has done that is through its volunteer program. GE employees volunteer more than one million hours of community service every year, learning about opportunities through GE's online Volunteer Portal.

The GE Volunteers of Greater Boston, for example, has supported the Food Project North Shore for more than three years. The project, which produces organic food on one acre of reclaimed urban land in Lynn, Massachusetts, donates more than 45,000 servings of vegetables to families in need through My Brother's Table and other pantries each year. GE Volunteers also educates 170 children at Ingalls Elementary School about land use and nutrition and provides internships for 40 high school students.

Volunteers in the chapter provide the labor and funding to keep and improve the land, plant the crops in the spring, and harvest them in the fall. All told, more than 100 volunteers donate 400 hours each year. That comes out to four hours per person—not an overwhelming commitment, but enough to make an enormous difference.

PricewaterhouseCoopers recently launched Earn Your Future, a $160 million commitment to advance responsible financial literacy aimed at reaching more than 2.5 million students in grades 3 to 12 and teachers in the United States. Employees volunteer in classrooms to teach the firm's free curriculum, which covers a variety of subjects including saving and investing, planning, and money management. The firm also provides free training to teachers on the subject. "To us, this commitment is about making a measurable impact in the marketplace through our people, but it is also about engaging our employees in a meaningful way," says Shannon Schuyler, the firm's corporate responsibility leader.

Here are some findings from an interesting study that you might use to convince your employer to offer a volunteer program for you and your colleagues. Companies that offer strong volunteer programs can increase their average revenue per participating employee by $2,500, according to a new study from CEB (cebglobal.com), an advisory group. The study, the first of its kind that I've heard of that puts a dollar value on corporate volunteer programs, shows that these programs can ramp up employee engagement levels by 8 percent and significantly reduce employee turnover.

"Employee participation rates in corporate volunteer programs have been steadily rising over the past few years, but there is a lot of room for improvement," says Jennifer Lawson, vice president of corporate strategy at Points of Light, the volunteer organization that partnered with CEB in the research.

Be a Mentor or Sponsor

Mentoring and sponsoring are two other great ways to give back and add another dimension to your work life. Your employer may have opportunities for you to mentor someone in your office. Many employers have a formal or informal mentoring program. Big corporations such as American Express, Cisco, Citi, Deloitte, Ernst & Young, General Mills, Intel, Morgan Stanley, and Procter & Gamble, for example, all have mentoring and sponsorship programs.

Or keep an eye out for someone at work who you sense could use your support. Kate White, former editor of *Cosmopolitan* and author of *I Shouldn't Be Telling You This: Success Secrets Every Gutsy Girl Should Know,* shared her advice with me when I interviewed her for my column "Route 360," which runs on the PBS Next Avenue web site (nextavenue.org).

White says you can sense when young people you've worked with or know informally are looking for a hand to help direct them. "They are probably eager for mentoring, but don't know how to say it," she says, "and you just make that first gesture."

If it's been a while since White last saw the young woman she mentors, she might invite her to come over to her home for a glass of wine to catch up.

"It's good to keep a certain amount of face-to-face time with women you mentor because that gives them the opportunity to ask questions they might feel uncomfortable about by e-mail," says White. She also sends her mentees e-mails periodically to check in informally. And she makes sure the women she mentors don't feel shy about contacting her outside of the firm if they have a specific question or are worried about something and need her advice right then.

Or if you're in a position to do so, consider sponsoring someone, rather than mentoring. "The Sponsor Effect: Breaking through the Last Glass Ceiling," a study by the Center for Work-Life Policy, describes a sponsor as someone who "uses chips on his or her protégé's behalf and advocates for his or her next promotion as well as doing at least two of the following: expanding the perception of what the protégé can do; making connections to senior leaders; promoting his or her visibility; opening up career opportunities; offering advice on appearance and executive presence; making connections outside the company; and giving advice. Mentors proffer friendly advice. Sponsors pull you up to the next level."

Sylvia Ann Hewlett, an economist and author of *Forget a Mentor, Find a Sponsor* and *Executive Presence,* is a firm believer in sponsorships. Her advice: Don't take on too many sponsorees, no more than two or three. "These are people I feel have special promise that I invest it in, in major ways," she says. "You need to believe in them and see their value. There's a certain amount of risk in that. You're aligning your reputation with them. They're going to be walking around with your brand on them."

Once you've selected whom to mentor, Hewlett says, aggressively promote their careers. If they work for you or with you, "have them in mind when a stretch opportunity comes up," notes Hewlett. When promotions or raises are being discussed among managers, recommend that your sponsorees receive them.

And here's a dividend: Sponsoring can enhance your own career, according to Hewlett's studies. Leaders who sponsor two or three high-performing talents progress faster themselves.

Outside Mentoring Opportunities

You might also look for mentoring prospects outside of your workplace. I recently discovered a nonprofit veterans mentoring program, American Corporate Partners (acp-usa.org), dedicated to assisting veterans in their transition from the armed services to the civilian workforce. Finding a job is tough for veterans for a variety of reasons, including the simple struggle for vets to translate their military service skills to the civilian workplace.

With the mentoring guidance of business professionals nationwide, ACP offers veterans tools for career growth through mentoring, career counseling, and networking opportunities. Much of the advice is parlayed via an online bulletin board where HR experts and seasoned professionals give advice in response to specific workplace and education questions posed by military vets of all ranks, stripes, and ages.

ACP's mentoring program is open to all currently serving and recently separated veterans (including members of the Reserve and National Guard) who have served on active duty for at least 180 days since September 11, 2001, according to the web site. ACP's mentoring program is also open to spouses of veterans killed on duty and spouses of severely wounded post-9/11 veterans.

Unlike traditional "wisdom of the crowd" sites like Yahoo! Answers or Ask.com, the volunteer contributors on ACP's bulletin board are highly credentialed and vetted beforehand. IBM employees created the web site's online bulletin board and app on a pro bono basis.

ACP also pairs specific vets with corporate execs in more traditional mentor-protégé relationships. Although the initial effort was started by IBM, employees from corporations such as Alcoa, Bloomberg, Disney, PNC, UPS, and Yum! Brands now participate.

Another intriguing veteran mentoring group that works alongside corporations is Joining Forces Mentoring Plus (joiningforcesmentoringplus.org). The organization offers free personal coaching and professional guidance—including working-women mentors—for women veterans of all ranks and eras, military and veteran spouses, caregivers of wounded warriors, and survivors of fallen soldiers.

I'm a huge advocate of career mentoring, but I didn't know about Joining Forces Mentoring Plus until I heard a presentation by Mary Ann Sack at the recent Women's Institute for a Secure Retirement (WISER) Women's Retirement Symposium in Washington, D.C.

Sack is director of business development and programming at the Business and Professional Women's Foundation (bpwfoundation.org), the organization behind the mentoring program, which provides unlimited free online career development tools and resources to participants. Her passionate talk about the challenges these types of women face finding work—and the assistance Joining Forces Mentoring Plus has provided—really caught my attention.

The organization's goal: to build the Joining Forces Mentoring Plus community from its current 1,000 mentors and mentees to 5,000 over the next two years. Women who'd like to help out at Joining Forces Mentoring Plus can do so in a variety of ways.

If you want to offer your expertise occasionally, you could become a subject-matter expert. For instance, you might lend your services offering tips on rewriting a resume, negotiating a salary, or starting a business.

If you want to mentor through Joining Forces, you might be able to do so through your employer. The program has partnerships with more than 55 companies and organizations such as Citicorp, CVS

Caremark, and Intel. Otherwise, you can sign up on the Joining Forces Mentoring Plus web site.

But if you'd like to be a one-on-one mentor, prepare to make a serious commitment. "We are not looking for someone who is just interested in a six-month gig," said Sack. "We want to be forming relationships with these women that take them through their careers.

Another great example of a corporate mentoring program is the Michelin Challenge Education volunteer mentoring program, which helps students in struggling public elementary schools near Michelin's American plants. It provides support to public Title 1 elementary schools in the form of tutors, mentors, and lunch buddies. Michelin's Challenge Education program pairs employees with elementary schools to make presentations and provide tutoring on a range of subjects, including elementary physics; healthful eating; and basic math, science, and reading skills.

Big Brothers Big Sisters (bbbs.org) has been helping children—often those from single- or low-income households, or from families where a parent is incarcerated or serving in the military—with one-on-one mentoring relationships. Big Brothers Big Sisters makes monitored matches between adult volunteers ("Bigs") and children ("Littles") ages 6 through 18 in communities across the country. With nearly 340 agencies across the country, Big Brothers Big Sisters serves approximately 200,000 children, their families, and the 200,000 volunteer mentors who work with them.

Your high school or college alumni association may offer mentoring opportunities, too. Also, professional associations often pair younger members with experienced mentors. Your local Rotary Club and Chamber of Commerce are also good resources.

Another tactic is to find a mentee via a local college or university. Charlotte Beyer, founder and CEO of the Institute for Private Investors, has taken this path. She prefers to mentor young women in college.

She does just that at Hunter College of the City University of New York, where she mentors one student annually. "I'm continually inspired by these mentees, whom I stay in close touch with, even after our official year of mentoring," she says.

Hunter's management of its mentoring program is a key reason for its success. Mentees and mentors must apply to be involved and then attend an orientation, midyear check-in consultations, and a year-end evaluation reception. "A certain minimum time each month of face-to-face contact is expected and tracked," Beyer explains.

Her mentees are first-generation Americans whose families emigrated from India, Ukraine, and Siberia. "I feel it is an honor to mentor them—not giving advice so much as exposing them to the business world, helping them network toward a job or internship, and sharing stories from the real world," says Beyer.

My older sister, Pat, has reached out in a similar way. She is part of a Philadelphia high school mentor program that has a pretty rigorous acceptance process that includes background checks before you are assigned to a particular student.

Find Your Own Mentor or Sponsor

Then again, maybe you can recharge your work life by tapping your own mentor or sponsor. It really does pay to have someone at your back when it comes to getting ahead in the workplace. That mentor or sponsor can play several roles, from teaching to promoting your talents to others in the organization to encouraging you.

A study published by economist Hewlett found that both men and women who have a sponsor behind them are more likely to ask their boss for a "stretch" assignment and are more likely to ask for raises than those without one.

Asking someone for advice on one action or problem is the easiest way to begin this kind of relationship. It's a baby step and allows the relationship to grow over time. You do want to schedule regular meetings even if it is just to have a cup of coffee and touch base on how things are going. Mentorships and sponsorships frequently turn into a friendship. And both parties benefit. The main reason most mentors and sponsors say they take the time to counsel and help is the elusive gratification they get in paying it forward.

If you do decide to look for a mentor or sponsor, be clear about your goals for the relationship. Write them down in your journal to help you focus on what you hope to achieve. You might have a certain business task at hand, something as simple as wanting someone who is valued in your company to give you advice on how to spruce up your image in the workplace, such as proper attire. Or it could be someone who can guide you on the best way to ask for a salary bump or a new assignment. Or perhaps you're looking for someone who can, in essence, help you learn the ropes of a new business area or skill. Don't rule out a mentor younger than you, who can offer more experience and direction when it comes to areas like technology or social media where you might not feel quite as confident.

A less personal, but potentially helpful, mentor matchmaking firm is PivotPlanet (pivotplanet.com), which offers videoconference, phone, and in-person mentoring for individuals for a fee. (It also offers Pivot Enterprise, a platform that universities, large nonprofits, and companies use to connect employees and alumni with subject-matter experts. Check with your HR department or alumni association to see if it is offered to you free as a benefit; if not, ask if your organization or alma mater might consider it.) I've used the individual services of one of its mentors, who lives in Florida, hundreds of miles from my home in Washington, D.C., to hone my public speaking goals and business plan. I found my one-on-one sessions incredibly useful and empowering, and the $180 fee well worth it.

Adding Value to Your Job

Beyond volunteering, mentoring, and sponsoring, how can you tweak your current job, working around the edges to give it new life? Here are eight moves to consider:

1. *Get up to speed on your industry.* It's easy to get complacent about staying current with the trends in your specific field. That's risky. You get left behind, and when new opportunities arise, you aren't nimble enough to notice what's on the horizon or prepared to step into new roles or assignments. Make a practice of reading trade publications. Set up a Google Alert to notify you when your employer is in the news, or when one of its competitors is making waves or launching a new venture. Just being in the know can inspire you to think of projects and tasks you might be able to volunteer for or

to get involved in starting. At the very least, you will be able to engage in knowledgeable discussions with your boss and coworkers about your firm and its current and future challenges.

2. *Do some sleuthing.* Dissect your current position to pinpoint a new responsibility you can add that will refresh your focus, and maybe even scare you a little bit. Keep your ear to the ground and try to get the scoop on positions opening up, or a new project that's on the cusp of starting—even if it is just a short-term one. Your supervisor might not be super-excited about giving you the chance to try something new, but it's worth throwing your name into the hat, if it is something you think you can handle and are qualified to take on. (More on how to have this conversation in Chapter 8.)

3. *Ask for new duties.* You've probably heard the definition of insanity: doing the same thing over and over again but expecting different results. If you're constantly doing the same set of tasks each day, the monotony alone can suck you down. So step it up. Probably no one else is going to change that for you. You have to be out front and request to be considered for new projects. What is it that you would like to do? How can you move in this direction?

   It starts with feeling confident that you can take on these new duties. As Norman Vincent Peale once said: "Believe in yourself. Have faith in your abilities. Without a humble but reasonable confidence in your powers, you cannot be successful or happy." Or as hockey great Wayne Gretzky said, "You miss 100 percent of the shots you don't take." Or as my niece's high school basketball coach used to shout at the girls from the sidelines, "You can't make 'em if you don't take 'em."

4. *Say yes to new responsibilities.* If you're asked to do something and you're worried you aren't up to the task, my advice is to accept the invitation gracefully and with confidence, and then get moving to figure out how to do it. The adrenaline alone will charge you up. And when you succeed, the rewards will be both internal and external.

5. *Ramp up the work you like to do.* Consider what facets of your job you really do appreciate and are good at (you uncovered these in your MRI), and then concentrate on increasing those activities.

6. *Investigate openings at your employer's other office locations.* This isn't a move that will suit everyone, but it definitely is worth exploring for those of you who are nimble and not tied down with families and young children in school. When you move to an entirely different office with new coworkers, that "new kid on the block" experience can be a blast both professionally and personally. And that change can make all the difference in how you approach your job.

7. *Adjust how you connect with your coworkers.* Subtle changes in your own behavior each day can have a huge impact.

   • *Step away from your me-me-me complex.* The mission is to stop talking about yourself and complaining. It reflects badly on you and rarely results in change. Instead, practice listening and supporting your coworkers.

   • *Reach out to new colleagues or those you don't know well.* Ask someone you don't really know to grab lunch and learn about what they do and their background. Set a goal to do this kind of outreach at least once or twice a month. Or create games at work that provide ways to open up and connect. You might start a weekly card game during lunch, for instance.

   • *Make eye contact with your coworkers.* Sounds simple. But pay attention. Do you? New scientific evidence suggests that if you don't make direct eye contact with coworkers, you're at a distinct disadvantage in trying to figure out what they really feel or mean. And it's easy for misunderstandings and resentments to develop. Accessing this emotion makes you wiser and can do wonders in improving your workplace relationships.

   • *Add more face time.* When you're physically and emotionally present to others at work, it sparks energy and a feeling of fellowship and camaraderie. So slow down. Pause every so often. Maybe all you need to do is stop by someone's office to talk about something that's not work related, or offer to grab an extra cup of coffee from the lunchroom if you're headed that way and drop it off at a colleague's desk. Instead of e-mailing your reply or calling someone back, have a face-to-face chat.

- *Laugh more.* A recent Gallup poll found that people who smile and laugh at work are more engaged in their jobs. And the more engaged you are, the happier and more enthusiastic you will be. It will not only trickle down to the quality of your work; people will also want what you have. You will be the one they seek out to have on their team. To quote Maya Angelou, "If you don't like something, change it. If you can't change it, change your attitude."

8. *Adjust how you connect with your boss.* Employees say that their bosses and direct supervisors are key when it comes to job satisfaction and engagement, according to the 2013 global workforce index survey by Kelly Services Inc.

   The survey found that 61 percent of respondents in the United States believe their direct manager or supervisor has a significant impact on their job satisfaction or engagement. (More than 120,000 respondents in 31 countries participated in the survey, including more than 18,000 in the United States.)

   "It is sometimes said that employees don't leave companies, they leave managers," said Steve Armstrong, senior vice president and general manager of U.S. Operations for Kelly Services.

   Here are my six tips for coping with a tough boss:

   - *Keep your eyes on your work.* No matter how difficult your boss is, keep your side of the street clean. If your unhappiness with him impacts your work output in any way, and you let it affect your productivity, or start withdrawing or calling in sick, that will come back to bite *you,* not him. Your work is your reputation.
   - *Anticipate what's next.* Make it your mission to do what you say you'll do, get your projects done ahead of time, and show up when you say you will so your boss isn't compelled to ride you and look over your shoulder, fretting that you

will not deliver on schedule. No one wants to be micro-managed. Start building that trust now, and maintain it day in and day out, so your boss knows he or she can count on you.

- *Write it down.* When you're grappling with a tough boss, keep a paper trail of your interactions, especially if there are unreasonable requests or critiques of your work that you feel are unwarranted. Immediately write down the day, the issue, and why you disagree with your boss's inter-pretation. Write down all the good stuff, too—when she praises you or your work wins awards or recognition from higher-ups or clients. If you're given a verbal request for something, write an e-mail back to your boss to be sure you're clear on the assignment. There is no room for miscommunication when you're working with a mercu-rial manager.

- *Play your poker face.* Skip the drama. Patience is the name of the game when your boss ticks you off or does something so egregious that your head is spinning. Take a breath. Do not fire off an e-mail or start grumbling aloud about it with your coworkers. Take the high road. It might blow over. When the tension calms down, you can have a discussion with your boss about the matter in a less reactive, more level-headed fashion.

- *Get to know him.* It helps to have a bead on what he really cares about and what sets him off. Sometimes it's how something looks to others rather than what you actually did. Maybe inside he thinks it's fine for you to work from home one day a week, but he's worried about how it looks to his boss or the other people he manages. Or perhaps your boss is a stickler for being on time to work. If tardiness builds resentment every time you slide in 15 minutes past 8 A.M., cut it out. Get to work on time. Make every effort to play by his rules. When you open the door with one small annoyance, the floodgates can swing wide, and you become fair game for closer scrutiny and potential criticisms. These are meltdowns you can easily sidestep with a little discipline and understanding of human psychology on your part.

A YOUNGER BOSS GOT YOU DOWN? 10 SURVIVAL TIPS

Here's another workplace downer that no one really wants to address. But face it. One of the latest challenges for older workers is figuring out how to work effectively and happily for a boss who is younger.

Many of us these days already have one—or we will. As more Boomers push back retirement dates, and working part time becomes a pillar of our retirement, this generational dance is taking place in small and large businesses across the country.

A survey by the jobs web site CareerBuilder found that one-third of employees in the United States reported working for someone younger. Fifteen percent said their boss was at least 10 years younger.

While most workers said it wasn't difficult to work for a younger boss, differences in work styles and communication often cropped up. The truth is that even if your boss is razor sharp and has the chops to lead, it's tough not to chafe when taking orders from someone who's the same age as your kids.

Here are 10 ways to help you deal with the age difference.

1. *Manage your attitude.* Keep in mind that you were once that brash young boss or rising star, full of clever ideas and new ways of doing things. So listen carefully to what the boss has to say and respect the title and position. "Go out of your way to show your willingness to try new approaches," says Beverly Jones, the executive career coach in Washington, D.C.

   According to the CareerBuilder survey, some employees complained that their younger bosses acted as if they knew more than older workers when they didn't. That may be true in some cases, but don't be so certain that you know more. You don't want to come across as a know-it-all. So quiet the condescending tone in your voice. How you treat someone, even subliminally, generally is reflected back at you.

Beware of developing a repetitive negative thought, like "What does he know? He's got no experience," Jones says. "Reframe your thinking, and regularly repeat a positive reminder to yourself, like 'He's the boss. I'll figure out what he wants and needs, and I'll give it to him.'"

Then, too, try to see it from your boss's perspective. While you're fretting that your expertise isn't valued, your supervisor may in fact be bristling that you're acting like a parent or mentor, and not giving proper credit for his or her education and experience.

2. *Talk about the elephant in the room.* Younger bosses may wonder if you will have a tough time reporting to someone their age. They're concerned that you're set in your ways, not willing to try new approaches to doing things, not up to snuff with technology, and possibly you don't have the grit to do the job. Tell them you realize that they may have these concerns, but explain why they shouldn't worry. Better yet, show them.

   "Get social," Jones says. "You may not feel like hanging out with younger coworkers, but do it anyway, at least sometimes. Connecting at casual events can help you build vital relationships and it will keep you in the information loop." If it's appropriate for your position, stay engaged on social networks such as LinkedIn industry groups, Google+, or Twitter by posting interesting articles. You could forward an article to your boss that you think is cutting edge with a note that you ran across it via one of your social media platforms.

3. *Concentrate on what you have to offer.* "It's important for the more experienced worker to try to focus on what he or she offers the employer rather than overly focusing on the age concern," says Miriam Salpeter, a job search consultant at Keppie Careers and author of a new free e-book, *5 Mistakes Job Seekers Make and How to Avoid Them.* "Consider your experience an asset and pay attention to how well you're prepared to do the job. For example,

(continued)

91

your maturity and experience helps you solve problems more quickly." Volunteer to mentor younger workers or be mentored by younger colleagues in areas where your boss may show some concern about your prowess.

4. *Find the silver lining.* The enthusiasm that a younger boss brings to the job can be contagious. Soak it up. "If you've ever managed other people, you know it can be hard work," says Michelle Hynes, a career coach in Portland, Oregon. "Your supervisor will love you if you're one of the people who makes it easy—and even fun."

Be positive. "Cross-generational misunderstandings can arise in any relationship," Hynes says. "But staying open to new learning, asking questions when something goes awry, and genuinely wanting a win-win situation will go a long way."

The key to success in a younger-boss scenario? "Realize that you're building a relationship that allows each of you to be successful in the workplace," Hynes says. "Ask yourself: How can I be a good partner?"

And be curious, she advises: "Everyone's experience has limits, and there's always more to learn. What growth opportunities does working with and for this person offer?"

Finally, be generous. "You have knowledge and networks built over many decades," she says. "How can sharing these help your boss succeed?"

5. *Get hip to texting.* A younger manager will probably want to communicate with you via e-mail or, better yet, text message rather than through face-to-face chats or the phone. Voice messages are passé. For the younger set, a missed cell phone call is an ignored cell phone call. Don't resist. It's up to you to adapt.

6. *Prepare for less face time.* For many younger managers, time spent in the office is not as vital as the results you produce. So your well-honed work ethic of being an early bird at your desk might not impress. The new regime

may look more favorably on teleworking, especially if you can get more work done by not cooling your heels in rush-hour commutes.

Meetings are more likely to be via teleconferences and webinars. Get acquainted with Web-based applications like Cisco WebEx, Google+ Hangouts, GoToMeeting, Join.me, and TeamViewer. See which platform your company or IT department prefers. If you haven't tried it at work, get comfortable by trying these platforms with someone outside the office.

7. *Note your latest achievements.* "Let go of the past," Jones says. "It's great to feel pride for accomplishments in past years, but know that you get no points for them in today's workplace. Your boss is focused on current challenges and wants to know regularly how you're helping to address today's problems and tomorrow's goals."

8. *Steer away from age-centric comments.* Avoid suggesting that something younger managers do is similar to something your adult children are doing, or bringing up what you were doing when you were their age. This sounds obvious, but sometimes it slips out because you're thinking it. Your boss rarely wants to know that he or she reminds you of your child.

And skip the chitchat about your personal life that dates you. For example, Salpeter says, "There's no need to bring up the fact that you're expecting your third grandchild."

9. *Keep your skills current.* If you've recently updated any software certifications or you are proficient in social media, let your boss know. Ask to take advantage of retraining opportunities to keep your entire tool kit sharp. You might also ask if you can take an online course or weekend workshop that will pump up your performance in some way. Maybe your company's tuition reimbursement program will pay for it.

(continued)

"Embrace new ways," Jones says. "A young boss may assume that an older worker is resistant to change. Show it ain't so. Make it your business to learn new technologies and stay up to date on industry trends. Your age will be irrelevant if your skills are fresh and your focus is on the future."

10. *Don't act old.* If you look and sound over the hill, your younger boss may assume your job skills are dated as well, Jones says. Pay attention to what comes out of your mouth. Do you persistently complain about your achy back, remind folks how things were handled back in the day, or habitually refer to your age? "If so, you're the one making age an issue," she says.

Consider a style makeover, Jones says. Spruce up your wardrobe and hair to give them a fresh, updated look. Free personal shoppers are available at many department stores to help, or you can ask friends for tips.

And you might consider a mini-makeover. You don't necessarily need to dye your hair or spring for Botox or a chemical peel for your face, but there are things you can do to have a more youthful glow. If you aren't physically fit, for instance, make that a priority and eat healthfully.

When you're in shape and feel good about yourself, you have a certain vitality and oomph that people want to be around, regardless of your age. It subtly says, "I'm up for the job, bring it on."

Take Control of Your Time

As you did earlier in this book, where you jotted down what you did each day, now it's time to really key in on the activities you get the most bang out of personally and professionally and those that just suck up your time. Focusing will help you better enjoy your time on the job.

Keep a log of your hour-by-hour actions for two or three weeks. Which ones were worth it in terms of your work and your personal satisfaction? Are there ways to pare away the ones that dragged you down?

Cut Back on Interruptions

Working hard is critical, but it's not about putting in the hours. Working smart means making a concentrated effort without distractions. As Thomas Jefferson said, "I'm a great believer in luck. And I find the harder I work, the more I have of it."

Find ways to stay focused. When I have an assignment due, I turn off my cell phone and the sound on my computer, silencing the ding of in-coming e-mails. I don't work in an office, so I rarely have to contend with coworkers popping by. If you do, find a way to close your door periodically. Maybe put a sign up that you're not to be disturbed for the next half hour or some appropriate time period. You might have to get your boss to okay the time-out, but my guess is that if it ups your productivity and quality of your work, your supervisor will be all for it.

If you're like me, once you are distracted, it takes time to get back into the work at hand, and sometimes you really never can get the rhythm rolling. And that loss of that zone in itself makes you feel lousy, frustrated, and stressed out.

Learn to Delegate

Step away from the minutiae, if your work allows it. You may not have to do it all. Are you a control freak? Take a good look at your personal work behavior. Perhaps some of these time zappers could easily be done by someone junior without the world collapsing—or perhaps they can even be eliminated all together. Write a list for a month of all these kinds of mindless small tasks you do day in and day out, and see how you can strip it down to free you up for more productive and less mind-numbing work. If you work on your own, you might need to budget the funds needed to hire an intern part time or a virtual assistant.

Stop Stalling

Seriously, procrastination is a losing proposition for you and for those who are depending on you to deliver the goods. Learn to recognize its signs. It might be that you click onto a news story to read online, and that leads to another link and then another. Or you pop out to grab a cool drink, or suddenly you remember a personal call you need to make pronto. Depending on where your office is or how vigilant your boss is, you might give yourself permission to get sidetracked by posting on Twitter or Facebook or returning e-mails. (E-mails, by the way, are the easiest to control. These little escapes can cost you. You might try setting aside a specific time each day for responding to or deleting e-mails all at the same time. This tactic, however, takes discipline, and some missives demand immediate attention.)

The trick is to find a way to reward yourself for tackling an assignment that you're trying to avoid. For me, it might be that if I get this article written or this batch of e-mails returned, I can take my dog for a 45-minute walk and get some fresh air. Plus, she inevitably makes me smile. With that in mind, I can usually buckle down and focus.

Get Involved in "Extracurricular" Activities

Take time out for yourself. Activities outside of work might range from reading to cooking to exercise, according to research conducted and presented at the Work and Family Researchers Network Conference in New York City by Eunae Cho, an assistant professor in psychology at the State University of New York at Albany. Cho found that workers who take time out for themselves—any kind of time out—are happier, feel more relaxed, and have increased vitality. That will spill over into your work life. When you participate in sports or exercise, cooking, lawn care, or even managing your investments, it shifts your mind-set to a completely different arena and gives you a sense of gratification, accomplishment, and achievement. While she focused on married women, the results can be applied to both sexes.

Here are some areas to explore that take place outside the office but can potentially have a workplace connection that will build workplace happiness.

- Got a musical bent? Form a band with a group of coworkers to play music, or if you can carry a tune, start an a cappella group. Maybe you can arrange to play gigs gratis at area assisted living and nursing homes or hospices. The National Institutes of Health, for example, has the NIH orchestra, drawing on the musical talents of its staff around Bethesda, Maryland. Marsh & McLennan Companies, a global professional services firm, has an employee choir, The MMC Chorale.

- Start a book club.
- Enroll in fitness, dance, yoga, or meditation classes. Some employers offer these classes in their on-site fitness centers. If not, ask if you can start one.
- Join and engage in professional associations that are work-related but meet outside the office.
- Join or organize a company team sport—say, softball, kickball, or bowling.
- Get involved in your alumni associations. See if anyone else at work went to your alma mater and form a lunch or discussion group or join them to watch televised sporting events. Plan to attend alumni events together.
- Participate in nonprofit board work with a group, even your alma mater, whose mission is close to your heart.
- Form a community gardening group. Perhaps your employer will provide space on its property, or one member might volunteer a plot at her or his home that everyone can participate in planning for and nurturing.
- Sign up for continuing education or professional development programs offered by your employer (more about this in Chapter 7).
- Start or join a walking, biking, or running group with coworkers at lunchtime, after hours, or on weekends.
- Check into your company perks. Chesapeake Energy Corporation, one of the nation's biggest natural gas producers, for example, offers free SCUBA certification to all its employees. Its on-site, 72,000-square-foot fitness center includes an Olympic-size pool, a sand volleyball court, a rock-climbing wall, and a quarter-mile walking track.
- Plan a vacation and ask coworkers for their input or suggestions.

Chapter Recap

In this chapter, we looked at a smorgasbord of ways to find renewal and joy around the edges of our working life. That feeling might bubble up from volunteering activities whether or not it is organized through your employer, or from mentoring someone or being mentored, or sponsoring a colleague. We explored ways to expand your working activities while on the job, how to recognize workplace dynamics that are sucking the wind out of your sails, and the power of reconnecting and caring about your coworkers in building workplace goodwill and creating a healthier "people" environment.

Your To-Do List

- Check to see if your employer sponsors volunteer projects.
- Investigate mentoring and sponsoring opportunities both in and out of work.
- Write down a list of reasons that you want a mentor and your goals for that relationship.
- Seek out your own mentor.
- Think about your relationship with your boss, and adjust if necessary.
- For two weeks, keep a running tab in your Job Remodeling journal of how much time you spend on the tasks you do each workday, and jot down ways you could become more efficient.
- Make a list in your journal of "off-the-job" activities you'd love to do.

6

How to Build Flexibility into Your Job

■ ■ ■

It's Labor Day, and while many workers in the United States are savoring the extra day off, I'm working. But I'm not complaining. I'm perched in a comfy chair on the porch of a simple cottage overlooking a shimmering pond, a herd of horses, and the hazy blue Shenandoah Mountains in the distance. The morning mist is heavy, and I can hear a rooster proudly announcing the dawn.

Not a bad place to work. My commute? Less than 15 seconds. I run my own media business, and I make my office wherever my bootheels may be wandering, to paraphrase the line from Bob Dylan's "Mr. Tambourine Man." My work life is flexible, and my entire life is so much better since I quit working in an office as a journalist more than a decade ago. Plus, I'm more productive than I've ever been.

When I ask people to name one thing that would make them happier about their jobs, they say independence in some way, shape, or form. "Let me work from home a few days a week, or allow me to tap into flextime options," they say. The option to work flexibly gives us a sense of control and autonomy. And it lets us participate in the other activities we value in our lives.

I can't describe the joy it brings me not to have to ask anyone permission to head off for a midday horseback-riding lesson, walk my dog down the lane, meet a friend for coffee, or take a vacation (although I always work some of the time when I'm on the road, but that's okay with me, too; I love to write in the early morning hours).

And I smile as I type this sentence while those horses thunder by at a gallop in their grassy field. For me, that's the sweet sight (and sound) of having flexibility in my work life.

In this chapter, you will learn about various flexible work arrangements that you might be able to take advantage of and how to ask your boss if you can try it out. I will show you how and why you and your employer can benefit. I will also review the pros and cons of the various kinds of flexible work arrangements to give you a better understanding of how they work and whether or not such as arrangement might work for you and your employer.

Work Flexibility and Happiness

Before I dive into the pros and cons of building flexibility into your job—be it through telecommuting or other flexible work schedules—and why and how you and your employer can benefit, let me take a minute to give you the view from the top about the current state of workplace flexibility and telecommuting.

The appeal of working from home, or remotely, whether full time or part time, is easy to understand. As I have said, it gives us a sense of autonomy and control of our time. When it comes to what makes people love their jobs, this is a biggie. Telecommuting employees are happier and more loyal, and they have fewer unscheduled absences, according to a survey by outplacement firm Challenger, Gray & Christmas. My research and interviews with hundreds of workers have clearly shown that more flexibility in scheduling day-to-day activities leads to greater happiness on the job. That's especially true as you get older.

According to Cali Williams Yost, an expert on managing work and life and author of *Tweak It: Make What Matters to You Happen Every Day* (Tweakittogether.com and http://worklifefit.com/blog/), "When you pass the 50th birthday milestone, the appeal of working more flexibly may begin to grow. You might wonder: 'Instead of enduring a two-hour, round-trip commute every day, maybe I could I work from home two days a week and devote a portion of the 10 hours I save to volunteer work.' Or: 'Rather than retiring completely, perhaps I could reduce my schedule and continue to contribute at work.'"

And remember, it's not always about the money, honey. In a recent study of "outstandingly engaged business units" by Susan David, a founder of the Harvard/McLean Institute of Coaching and a faculty member at Harvard, she asked what drove people to be highly engaged a work, and only 4 percent of respondents mentioned pay. Instead, they highlighted feeling autonomous and empowered, and a sense of belonging on their teams. "The reality is that human needs can't be neatly arranged into a pyramid," according to David. "Motivation isn't simple, and it's certainly not linear. Different people are motivated by different things."

Well said. I have found that the allure of flextime is that it can go a long way to making you feel more engaged and take ownership of your work in a way that you don't when you're expected to report in and simply have your bottom in a seat. Working in an open newsroom, where nearly all the reporting was done via telephone or computer, drove me crazy. Heaven forbid you left your desk for lunch anywhere but in the company cafeteria. I felt that my boss didn't trust me to get my job done. (Whether he really did or not, I don't know because I never asked.) I felt watched and under a glass, and I let that resentment fester.

Now that I can work wherever and whenever I want, one of my clients is that same employer, and honestly, I'm excited about the articles I write for the paper, and my work is far better, in my opinion. One top editor there noted that I've published more now there than I did when I was on staff parked in my seat.

The managerial "control" had simply flipped my switch to off. So I can relate to how huge an impact having control over where and when you work can have on what you produce. When you take back control of your work life, and you succeed, "it's sick," as my niece would say, meaning crazy cool.

That said, there has been some pushback lately, and I would be remiss not to mention it here. Some big-name companies—including Best Buy, Hewlett-Packard, and Yahoo!—have either publicly jettisoned or sharply reduced telecommuting, citing the need for more teamwork and innovation that comes from people rubbing elbows on a regular basis and the potential for impromptu meetings.

Moreover, even where the arrangement may technically be on the books, managers don't always know how to manage people who aren't in the office. And some employers don't offer support or training on how to manage the day-to-day and formal work flexibility that meet your needs and the expectations of your job, says Yost.

A Myriad of Flextime Options

There are all kinds of variations on the flextime theme, many of which are seasonal. But even these perks can go a long way to improving employee attitudes and loyalty. When I worked for *Money* magazine in New York, for example, we could leave early on Fridays during the summer months—anywhere from noon to 2 P.M. I loved it, and I respected my employer for giving us that sweetener and trusting that we would be accountable for our work.

The most popular flexible arrangements are telecommuting, job sharing, phased retirement of older workers, and schedule shifting or flexible schedules. Some of these arrangements can be temporary, such as permitting you to shift your workday to end an hour earlier than usual to take your mom to a doctor's appointment. Others can be more permanent, such as negotiating for a four-day-a-week schedule.

Or perhaps there's a job-share available where you could be loaned to another department for a few months. If there's an employee out on leave, maybe you can fill that job in the interim. If it's flextime and a reduced schedule you're dreaming of, you might be able to pair up with a younger worker—perhaps a new parent—who is looking for flextime to pool efforts in a way that gets the job done and makes your employer happy at the same time.

Companies report a wide variety of such options. "My company grants flexible schedules in the summer to enable employees to care for out-of-school kids or enjoy the sunshine by working, say, from 7 A.M. to 3 P.M.," says Zeynep Ilgaz, cofounder and president of Confirm Biosciences and TestCountry.

"We encourage our people to work from home or find alternatives when it makes sense," Shannon Schuyler, corporate responsibility leader at the auditing giant PricewaterhouseCoopers, told me. "When done well, offering flexibility results in better job satisfaction and increased productivity, all while helping manage our overall environmental footprint."

Scripps Health, based in San Diego, earned AARP's former Best Employers for Workers Over 50 award eight times since 2004. Here's why: Scripps offers a number of alternative work arrangements, including a phased retirement program. Employees have the opportunity to gain new experience by working on temporary assignments in other departments, on team projects, and by having access to formal job rotation and mentoring programs.

Google allows many of its employees to establish their own work hours. At Microsoft, employees can opt for when to begin their day, as long as it's between 9 A.M. and 11 A.M., and many telecommute. Other large companies that champion telecommuting include American Express, Apple, Dell, the auditing firm KPMG, and Xerox. Overall, according to a June 2014 report from the U.S. Bureau of Labor, about a quarter of employed Americans work from home some hours each week. And Forrester Research predicts that telecommuting will rise to include 43 percent of workers in the United States by 2016. According to Global Workplace Analytics, 50 percent of the workforce currently have jobs that can be done from home.

Not all of us are in a position that permits this liberty, however. Many jobs demand that you be physically present. Classroom teachers, retail sales clerks, and assembly-line workers, for example, cannot realistically do their jobs anywhere but on-site. And if you're managing a cadre of workers, you probably need to be present. If you have to be on-site to perform your job, chances are slim you'll be able to transition to teleworking full time. But there are options for you, too. For example, you might be able to negotiate with your boss flexible hours or an occasional work-from-home day.

But many professional, technological, and scientific occupations are more likely to offer workers flexible options, studies have found. The accounting industry as a whole, for example, has been a groundbreaker in offering workplace flexibility. Ernst & Young, for instance, offers formal flexible work arrangements, which could be one of, or a combination of, the following: reduced or variable hours, compressed workweeks, short-term seasonal schedules, and telework, including working at home and other office locations.

The best work-at-home jobs are often those that demand a quiet space with few distractions. Web-based jobs in accounting, translation, sales, public relations, medical transcription, and customer service are some of the growing areas that I write about in my book, AARP's *Great Jobs for Everyone 50+*, and more are coming on stream all the time. Nonetheless, you should always be aware of the need to keep your people skills sharp.

A variation on teleworking is sharing desks or offices. Also called "hoteling," sharing desks and offices is gaining traction at numerous organizations, including federal government agencies such as the General Services Administration (GSA), the Patent and Trademark Office, and the Departments of Agriculture and Homeland Security. The Fish and Wildlife Service and the Broadcasting Board of Governors have pilot programs, too. Corporate converts include pharmaceutical firm GlaxoSmithKline and the consulting firms Deloitte and Accenture. The impetus: Cutting the soaring cost of office space in some cities. But, hey, that can be a win for unhappy employees who would benefit from being sent home.

At the GSA headquarters, hundreds of telecommuting employees participate in a desk-sharing program requiring employees to reserve their workstations either daily or weekly in advance. On days when they're physically in the office, employees bring in their laptops and plug into desks they have reserved through an online booking system, which includes maps of the building and e-mail reminders sent out before the reservations begin.

"It really changed dramatically how this agency works and collaborates," Komal Rasheed, 31, a senior adviser on policy and strategy at the agency, was quoted in a *New York Times* article as saying. She finds it "liberating and freeing," she said, to work at different desks throughout the agency and to connect with other workers no longer restrained to one specific desk.

To help the shared-desk program work, government agencies offer telework training sessions, and the GSA web site includes copious pages dedicated to how to use the new workstations, including etiquette guidelines for sharing desks.

How Is Flextime Working?

At the risk of bogging you down, I will share some of the latest research in the area of flex work. If the numbers start to bug you, just skip ahead to your action steps.

Clearly, one of the most meaningful sources of flexibility is the ability for you to have some control over *when* you work.

- More than three quarters of employers in the United States report allowing at least *some* workers to periodically change their starting and quitting times, although just a quarter of employers say that they allow *most* of their employees to do so, according to "Work-Life Balance and the Economics of Workplace Flexibility," a June 2014 report by the Council of Economic Advisers.
- A company that encourages work-life balance practices for its employees can boost productivity, according to a study of more than 700 firms in the United States, the United Kingdom, France, and Germany, the Council of Economics Advisors reported. The authors say that this correlation could be driven by a third factor—good management. Well-managed firms have higher productivity and tend to embrace flexible workplace practices.
- Eighty-one percent of 1,051 surveyed employers with 50 or more employees allow employees to periodically change their starting and quitting time, according to the 2014 National Study of Employers from the Families and Work Institute and the Society for Human Resource Management. And almost three-quarters supported those employees who occasionally want to work from home.
- If you work for a small company, you may have a better chance at wresting some control of your working day, according to the National Study of Employers. In 2014, a third of small employers were more likely than large employers to allow employees to change starting and quitting times within some range of hours, compared with just 20 percent of large employers, and 11 percent of small employers allow employees to work some regular paid hours at home occasionally, as opposed to 4 percent of large employers. Two-thirds of small employers give workers control over when to take breaks, compared to just over half of large employers, and more than half of small employers allow workers to return to work gradually after childbirth or adoption and take time off during the workday

to attend to important family or personal needs without loss of pay, compared with 37 percent and 36 percent of large employers, respectively.

- Twenty-nine percent of employers reported allowing some workers to share jobs, and 36 percent reported allowing at least some to move from full-time to part-time work and back again while remaining at the same position or level, according to the 2014 National Study of Employers. A much smaller percentage of firms allowed most or all employees to take advantage of these forms of flexibility.
- More than half of employers allowed at least some workers to phase into retirement by working reduced hours, and 18 percent allowed most or all of their employees to do so, according to the National Study of Employers.
- A Sloan Center on Aging and Work at Boston College study on flexible work arrangements found that only 20 percent of companies offered a variety of flexible options to most of their workers.

While more employers say they provide flexible work arrangements for their employees, I have discovered, not surprisingly, that it's squarely in your court to negotiate with a supporting supervisor. I will explain ways to do this later in this chapter. But be aware that what a company gives lip service to and what it actually does in practice can be miles apart. "A lot of the existing research assumes companies are flexible if they report that they are. The reality is very different," Sociologist Stephen Sweet, a co-author of the Sloan Center study told the *New York Times*.

LAWS THAT ENCOURAGE FLEXIBLE SCHEDULES AND DISCOURAGE RETALIATION

Workers may be hesitant to ask about their employer's flexible scheduling policies because they fear this request will reflect poorly on them or cause them to lose their job, according to a 2014 report by the Council of Economic Advisers.

One-fifth of American adults, and more than a third of working parents and caregivers, report that they believe they have been denied a promotion, a raise, or a new job because they needed a flexible work schedule, according to the report.

"Right to request" laws try to cut this discrimination. Some local and state governments in the United States have already implemented such laws, which mandate that employees can't be retaliated against for asking. In 2013, San Francisco passed the Family Friendly Workplace Ordinance, which allows workers to request flexible or predictable working arrangements to help meet their responsibilities caring for children, elderly parents, or relatives with serious health conditions.

Vermont also passed legislation that allows workers to request workplace flexibility for any reason. These laws place no obligation on the employer to accept the request; they only require employers to consider the requests, provide an explanation if the request is denied, and not retaliate against workers for making the request. Employers are able to deny requests that would negatively affect business performance or impose high business costs.

Other countries, including the United Kingdom, New Zealand, and Australia, have also adopted "right to request" laws. Mothers with caregiving responsibilities submit most of these requests, and in its early years of implementation, employers fully or partially accepted more than 80 percent of them, the Council of Economic Advisers report found. In the United Kingdom, for example, more than 90 percent of employers have flexible work arrangements in the workplace, up from 50 percent in 1999.

Employers in the United Kingdom have reportedly achieved business benefits from flexible work arrangements, including improved employee relations, better recruitment and retention, lower absenteeism, and increased productivity, and the law was recently expanded to cover all workers, regardless of parent or caregiver status. "The connection seems clear—'right to request' laws make it easier and more likely for employees to

(continued)

ask for and obtain flexible work arrangements," according to the researchers. "Flexible work arrangements can also lead to working environments better matched to employees' needs and a more productive workforce for employers."

In the United States, President Barack Obama signed a Presidential Memorandum in June 2014 urging every agency in the federal government, as much as possible, to expand flexible workplace policies and give federal workers the right to request a flexible work arrangement without fear of retaliation.

TOP COMPANIES FOR FLEX WORK

To get an idea of some companies that value flexible working arrangements, check out this list. The online job site FlexJobs (flexjobs.com) analyzed recent work-from-home job listings to determine the companies that posted the most opportunities from June 5 to July 5, 2014. (The group also produces an annual listing of 100 firms.) Based on data from over 25,000 companies, these were the top 25 employers with the most available at-home positions:

1. Kaplan
2. IBM
3. US-Reports
4. First Data
5. About.com
6. Connections Academy
7. SAP
8. Xerox
9. Dell
10. Apple
11. PAREXEL
12. Forest Laboratories
13. UnitedHealth Group

14. VMware
15. K12
16. Aetna
17. Overland Solutions, Inc.
18. Salesforce.com
19. Infor
20. ADP
21. Red Hat
22. Broadspire
23. U.S. Department of the Interior
24. Covance
25. Aon

Top industries offering remote work opportunities include health care, information technology, education, nonprofit and philanthropy, and sales and marketing. Job titles include sales representative, senior analyst, nurse case manager, account executive, Web or software developer, accountant, and virtual teacher.

"The demand for telecommuting is growing, as is the acknowledgment by employers that remote job options can help attract and retain the best candidates," Sara Sutton Fell, founder and CEO of FlexJobs, stated. "These 25 companies are at the forefront of this trend, and the list provides great insight into the variety and the quality of the employers that offer telecommuting options."

Is Telework for You?

The truth is there's no one-size-fits-all method to teleworking. Whether or not it works for you depends on such things as your disposition, your work style, your career ambition, the sort of job you do, and, of course, the corporate culture of your employer.

If you're thinking of asking your employer to change your working arrangement to one that involves telework, ask yourself these three questions:

1. *Is my job right for working from home?* The best telecommuting jobs are often ones that require a quiet space to research, read, and process information without distraction. Virtual work, for example, is a natural fit if your job is Web-based. Remote jobs also may work well if you're in accounting, sales, public relations, medical transcription, or customer service.

   Freelance and contract workers who work from a home office, of course, perform many of these jobs. By their very nature, these positions generally don't require the face time associated with hobnobbing around the office, supervising employees, or sitting in meetings.

2. *Am I hardwired for telework?* To work from home on a regular basis, you'll need to be organized, disciplined, have first-rate time management skills, and be a self-starter. You may find that you're working harder because it may be hard to ignore your bosses' or coworkers' phone calls and e-mails even when you should technically not be working—say, late at night or on weekends. It can be really hard to push back from the computer and call it a day. You'll need to be able to set firm boundaries between work and home.

   Can you cope with being all alone? When you work remotely, there's no one to ask the follow-up query or to directly contest your thinking. You may miss out on rich collaborations and brainstorming you get from simply being "in the room." This is Marissa Mayer's topmost argument against working from home.

   More subtly, you can't suss out body language during a telephone conference meeting. So not seeing your colleagues may stop you from understanding what's really going on.

3. *Can I technically make it work?* Your communication skills must be top-drawer. That means you'll need to be comfortable communicating via phone, e-mail, and videoconferencing. If you need to give presentations or do any training, you should get familiar with Web-based meeting programs.

   But it goes a little deeper than that. While you don't need to be an IT whiz, Luddites need not apply. Teleworkers need to navigate the inevitable technology snafus and troubleshoot. For the fritzes you can't solve, you will need to have a good relationship with someone in your employer's IT department who can lend a hand quickly. A boss isn't going to put up with recurring "technical difficulties." Freelancers should line up a tech buddy on speed-dial.

The Risks of Working at Home

When I was in my 20s and 30s, I genuinely loved going to an office, although I had carefully chosen a profession that allowed me to spend plenty of time outside of the office traveling and reporting stories around the globe.

Back in those early days, office life was fun and engaging. My peers and I went to lunch in packs whenever possible. We gossiped, complained about bosses, and celebrated our successes together. We often socialized outside the office on weekends, even sharing group beach houses. We went to Happy Hour together, danced at nightclubs after a late night closing a story that was going to print, and went to one another's weddings. And we had the chance to interact regularly with more experienced colleagues and to learn from them.

But as we grew older, we began to have families and other life priorities, our social networks changed, and the office vibe became something quite different. For many of us—me included—it lost its newness and magic. In many respects, it became a place to go to put in time. We had cut our teeth in our chosen professions, and we were now entrenched in the routine, while our lives outside of the office took off, with new expectations and new demands.

I recall dreading that sense of being trapped in a cubicle in a big open newsroom, many floors above the ground, talking into a mouthpiece and typing. I clearly remember that gut-sinking feeling when I needed to ask for approval (as I often did) to slip out for lunch beyond the "biosphere," as I nicknamed one former employer's vast news-gathering facility.

I steadily grew to hate my job, but not the work itself. There is a difference. So I quit. And my "job" improved almost overnight. I wonder whether I would have stayed there if my boss had allowed me to work from home, even one day a week. But that wasn't part of that organization's culture back then.

For myself and many of my friends and colleagues who also work at home now, deciding when to perform our jobs—be it starting at 5 A.M. or 10 P.M.—makes us feel more in charge, more alive, and more engaged. (A disclaimer: The cronies I canvassed are in their 50s and 60s, so they're generally not dealing with the parenting issues that often entangle the work-from-home debate.)

But working at home can be hazardous to your wealth and to your career. Despite research showing that, in general, flexible work practices lead to increased productivity, higher job satisfaction, and decreased turnover, the question lingers as to whether employees who take advantage of flexible work policies incur career penalties for doing so. The Korn/Ferry Institute finds that 60 percent of 300 respondents in a recent survey say telecommuting inhibits career growth.

You may miss out on promotions and subsequent raises if you are not front and center at the office, where your manager can get a better sense of how you're performing. Ultimately, that can domino into lower lifetime earnings and retirement savings. And be forewarned: Some people, whether they work for themselves or for an employer, ultimately find that working from home can turn into one of the things they *don't* like about their jobs. That's because without your even realizing it, your job can morph into your life. When that happens, it's hard to find the right balance between work, family, hobbies, and other activities that can nourish you.

You *can* get your mojo back and enjoy a good work-life balance and other positive results that can emerge from a flexible work schedule of some kind. But it requires that you take the time up front to learn how to manage the process—from your tech skills to your time, to how you stay connected with your supervisor, coworkers, and clients.

Here's a rundown of the major perils of working from home—at least part of the time—and how to avoid them.

Your Workday Has No Limits

I'm not always ecstatic about my work-at-home workday (and night). I clearly love what I do and it doesn't always feel like work, but it's easy to get sucked into being available to work any time, any day. If only my former bosses could see me now. I vividly recall how difficult it was to get myself to the office in time for an obligatory 9 A.M. staff meeting every Thursday. These days, however, I work far more hours than when I slogged it out in-house—but that's by choice, and I don't think it hurts the quality of my work. In fact, I believe, it has made it better. But that's not the case for everyone.

My advice: If you have the tendency to work too much, set a limit on your daily hours—and try not to go over it. Make a daily work schedule for yourself each morning and hold yourself to it. Try as hard as you can to stick to a time when you will turn the switch off for the day and push away from your desk. Ideally, you should have a workspace that's separate from your living area, so you really can shut the door.

Set a clear schedule and let your boss and colleagues know what it is. Otherwise, you could be inviting phone calls and e-mails late at night and on weekends. You need to set boundaries on your personal time.

From my experience, as I said earlier, to work from home on a regular basis you must be well organized, have good time management skills, and be a self-starter. Not everyone is hardwired that way. Be honest with yourself before you take the leap.

Your Rise to the Top Might Be Thwarted

Employers figure that you can't really manage others when you work from home. I think they're probably right on many levels. Being a boss means face time. But even getting promoted (and the bigger salary that goes with it) often gets tied up in the "out-of-sight, out-of-mind" phenomenon. It's an unspoken trade-off at some firms if you decide to work from home.

By nature, bosses tend to fret about not being able to control what you do with your time and their powerlessness to keep tabs on your whereabouts. (Coworker jealousy can be palpable, too, making you feel shut out.)

In some companies, everyone works from home, offering up a greater possibility of moving up the corporate ladder. But those are still pretty rare. My colleagues working from home full-time for one employer with one or more corporate offices agree that the inability to climb the ladder has been a tacit trade-off that came with telecommuting. "You can't expect to get promotions if you're not there," a 50-something female friend who has worked for a large insurer for 15 years told me. "I'm okay with that."

Ana Dutra, chief executive of Korn/Ferry Leadership and Talent Consulting, agrees that teleworking can have long-term effects. "While working at home can be beneficial for both companies and workers, it can also lead to 'invisibility' that can limit opportunities for career advancement," she says. "It is important for telecommuters to remain networked as closely as possible with peers and leaders in the office."

I've turned down the invitation to climb the editors' ranks because I knew it would be hard to be a manager while working from home. But I'm not troubled about this. That's because I've grown to realize that my definition of career success and job happiness doesn't mean moving up the masthead, taking on more responsibility, and being a boss. What's more, a job like that wouldn't suit my temperament.

"There is a perception that if you are not in the office, you are more likely to miss important meetings, get passed over for promotion, or get targeted for layoff in the event of a downsizing," says John A. Challenger, chief executive of Challenger, Gray & Christmas.

My advice: Make sure you put in face time with your employer and colleagues. Attend on-site meetings on a regular basis, show up for other office gatherings, and have lunch or coffee with virtual colleagues and bosses.

If you are transitioning into a full-time telework schedule, this is key to not slipping into the "out-of-sight, out-of-mind" syndrome and staying on good terms with your coworkers. You might agree to be on-site when projects are being launched or for other company initiatives. But even if there is a nonbusiness event, such as a coworker's retirement or promotion, show your support and your connection to your coworkers by attending.

You Miss the Friendships and Social Networking

I do, admittedly, miss the bonding, friendships, and chances to meet new people in an office. Those things seldom happen when you work from home. "Even when you go in for meetings, you never quite get that," one telecommuting friend told me, somewhat wistfully.

Working remotely full time may cause you to miss out on rich workplace relationships, extemporaneous thinking, brainstorming, and the collaboration you get from simply being present at meetings or chatting in the lunchroom. As much as you might be in touch via phone, e-mail, or videoconferencing, will you be able to pick up on some of those nonverbal communication cues and know exactly what your boss and coworkers expect of you?

You also need to keep in mind that some of your coworkers might resent your new working arrangement, particularly if their job isn't suitable for telework.

My advice: Talk with your boss and workmates whenever you can. And I do mean talk—not just sending an e-mail or text, which are so much less personal. Get out of the house and squeeze in an out-of-the-office lunch or coffee with colleagues and bosses. Coworkers can also be envious and resentful of your freedom. With a little effort to schmooze with them at the office, you can avoid the bad blood.

At the very least, every so often, make a phone call instead of shooting off an e-mail or a text. It can be a time-suck, but I think it helps build camaraderie and you might even pick up some fun office gossip.

"I often opt for a phone call rather than an e-mail," says a pal who's a telecommuting IBM sales executive. "I know not everyone appreciates the time zap, but I preface it by saying: 'It's a quick question.'" She thinks phone calls result in more honest responses than she'd get with e-mails. If possible, establish a preset, scheduled phone call with your supervisor weekly, or daily, as a check-in.

And network with colleagues in your company and industry electronically. For instance, get active on Twitter, Facebook, or LinkedIn groups that relate to your work, employer, alma mater, past employers, or other interests that you follow. It's key to comment on posts from others and add in your own two cents. It displays your expertise and gives you a virtual feeling of being connected to a community.

I interact so frequently with many of my writer pals and my editors by regular—often daily—e-mails and online posts that when we do see one another, it's as if we have been working side by side all along, especially if I see pictures from their vacations, kids, and so forth up on Facebook. It sounds a little strange, but it's true.

Your Retirement Savings Take a Hit

If you work from home for a traditional employer, your salary can languish as a result of a plateauing career, which can have a nasty ripple effect on your retirement savings. When your income doesn't rise, it's tougher to increase the amount you put into your 401(k) or a similar employer-sponsored savings plan every year. Your employer's match will be lower as a result, too.

When you work for yourself, continuing to set aside money for retirement is essential because you don't have an employer's plan to automatically set funds aside for you. (The good news is that the self-employed can qualify for very big retirement savings breaks.)

My advice: Constantly push yourself to save as much for retirement as you can. Don't forget: You have until April 15 each year to fund an individual retirement account. Currently, you can put in up to $6,500 if you're 50 or older; $5,500 if you're younger.

You're Penalized for Shifting to Working Later Hours

A recent study, "Morning Employees Are Perceived as Better Employees," by Kai Chi Yam, Ryan Fehr, and Christopher M. Barnes of the Department of Management and Organization at the Michael G. Foster School of Business, University of Washington, published in the *Journal of Applied Psychology* (June 2014), found that employees who started work earlier in the day were rated by their supervisors as more conscientious, and thus received higher performance ratings.

Research participants gave higher ratings of conscientiousness and performance to the 7 A.M.–3 P.M. employees than to the 11 A.M.–7 P.M. employees. "Compared to people who choose to work earlier in the day, people who choose to work later in the day are implicitly assumed to be less conscientious and less effective in their jobs," the researchers found.

My advice: Talk to other workers using flex hours at your company and try to get a sense of their experience and feedback from supervisors. If you have the chance to use flextime, it might be best to move your schedule early in the day rather than later. But if you really do work best later in the day, make that case to your supervisor and then show her the results.

You Ignore Your Tax Deductions

Set aside a specific place exclusively for work. You'll be able to deduct it from your taxes and it will help you psychologically. Although an estimated 26 million Americans have home offices, just 3.4 million taxpayers claim home-office deductions.

Many people with home offices miss the tax breaks because they're nervous the write-offs will spark a tax audit. That's not really the case these days. But you must file Form 8829, "Expenses for Business Use of Your Home." You can read all the home office rules in IRS Publication 587.

My advice: In general, to write off home-office outlays, you must use the "area" for work only and on a regular or constant basis, either as your primary place of business or as a setting to meet with clients or to do paperwork such as writing invoices, ordering supplies, and making phone calls. I suggest you snap a pic of the space, too, so you have a record in case the IRS is ever curious. Be sure to consult with your tax adviser.

(If you're a full-time employee at a business, you will only qualify for the deductions if the company doesn't provide you with an office within their workplace.)

You should be able to write off 100 percent of the costs associated exclusively with your home office—everything from work computers to office supplies. The other kind of deductible home-office expenses are "indirect" ones that are prorated, based on the size of your home office. These are things like your mortgage or rent, insurance, and utility bills.

If the square footage of your home office equals 10 percent of your home's totally interior size, typically you can claim 10 percent of these expenses. If that sounds like a lot of paperwork, the IRS offers a shortcut or "safe harbor" rule, which allows you to deduct $5 per square foot of your home office, with a maximum write-off of $1,500 (based on a maximum of 300 square feet). But you won't be able to depreciate the part of your home used for business if you go this route. If your write-offs would top $1,500 or your home office is bigger than 300 square feet, you can still claim your home-office deductions based on actual expenses.

You Don't Have the Proper Business Paperwork

If you're operating a small business out of your home, you will probably need the proper tax registrations and business and occupational licenses and permits from federal, state, and local governments to operate legally.

My advice: Check with the chamber of commerce where you live to find out what is expected.

You Neglect to Buy Insurance

If you're operating a home business, it's probably a good idea to get an insurance rider in case the FedEx man trips. Most home-business owners have little or no coverage from their homeowner's policy. What's more, if you file a homeowner's (or renter's) claim for losses that stemmed from an undisclosed home-based business, your insurer may not cover it. If you have valuable equipment, you might want to protect it from theft or damage as well.

My advice: Each state sets its own rules about the insurance coverage that can be offered to home-based businesses. The least expensive way to add insurance is to tack on a rider to your existing homeowner's or renter's insurance policy. The cost might be around $100 a year for around $2,500 of additional coverage. For more, go to the Insurance Information Institute in New York City, an industry trade group and information clearinghouse.

You Forget to Pay Your Quarterly Taxes If You're Self-Employed

Ugh. It's quarterly tax time again. I know that dreaded feeling. Still, send in that check to avoid a possible penalty from the IRS for underpayment of taxes. Independent contractors who are paid only for work performed, in general, must pay federal taxes and FICA on their income. You will need to pay estimated taxes throughout the year instead of once a year on April 15.

My advice: Go to the Self-Employed Individual Tax Center on the IRS web site (irs.gov) to help you understand how to pay federal taxes as an independent contractor. Depending on the location of your business, you may be required to file state and local income and business taxes as well.

One last thought about working from home: To paraphrase the poet John Donne, "No man (or woman) is an island." The best work is collaborative. As much as I love being independent, I'm well aware that my work shines brightest after it has been touched by the inspiration of another, wherever that person is, at home or in the office.

Chapter Recap

In this chapter, we discussed how working a flexible schedule either by teleworking from your home office, shifting your hours, job sharing, and working compressed workweeks might deliver the energy and engagement that eludes you today. When you feel trapped and micromanaged in your office environment, the sense of control of your own time and virtual freedom can do wonders to help you get reconnected with your work again.

We reviewed efforts by various employers and federal and state governments to implement policies that prohibit companies from

A FLEXTIME CHECKLIST

- Talk to your boss or human resources department to see if your employer has a formal policy for allowing flexible schedules.
- Talk to other workers you know who have a flexible arrangement to get their view of the pros and cons.
- Draft a proposal that describes what your work schedule would be, the number of hours you would work, how unplanned overtime would be handled, how often you would check in with an office visit, and other issues.
- Request a trial period of three to six months so both you and your boss can see how the arrangement works out and tweak if necessary.

penalizing workers who request flexibility. Importantly, we reviewed the perils of flexible work options, and learned ways to steer clear of those potential hazards to make the arrangement a success for both you and your employer, or for your clients if you work for yourself.

Your To-Do List

- Evaluate your list of priorities for work-life balance. You can always revise later.
- Write down in your Job Remodeling journal why having flexibility at work will enhance your life and how it will make you more valuable to your employer.
- Review your job MRI to see if this kind of flexibility suits your temperament and goals.
- Talk to other employees who have an arrangement that you'd like to have.
- Draft a proposal to present to your boss.

7

How to Upgrade Your Game

■ ■ ■

When Adam Bryant, a reporter for *The New York Times,* asked Kat Cole, president of Cinnabon, what advice she gives to employees who are ambitious and want to move up, her answer did not surprise me. "Take your development into your own hands and be curious about the entire company," she responded. "If there's something you want to learn, go learn it."

That practical, hands-on approach can open doors to a potential promotion or lateral move—but more than that, it can ramp up your personal enthusiasm and curiosity about your job and push it in new directions. Learning is inner power. But it's up to you to take the initiative.

In this chapter, we probe ways to get back in the game intellectually and pick up new skills. You will find that "learning" doesn't even have to be directly related to your job for it to make you view your work from a different perspective. I attend lectures. I travel to new places as often as I can. I recently took an eight-week online course, "A Beginner's Guide to Irrational Behavior," that had nothing to do with my current job—or so I thought. But these types of activities enrich me in ways that trickle down.

How about you? Write down in your journal all the activities you participate in that spark your brain cells. Go deep. I bet you'll surprise yourself by how subtle your yearning to learn has been and how, without even realizing it, you've been feeding it.

The Benefits of Learning New Tricks

The inner implications of learning are critical to your happiness on the job and in your life. Learning shifts your brain. It gives you energy and confidence. The most creative and resilient professionals tend to engage regularly in learning or self-development efforts.

Many aging experts say that to stay healthy, you have to learn new things. When you stop challenging your brain with new experiences, you could be in trouble. Your skills can atrophy and a kind of depression can creep in.

Look around you at the people you admire. Think about the role models you had when you were younger and starting out in your career. No doubt, they were always curious and pushing themselves. My role model is my dad, who even at the age of 85, was pushing to learn about robotics and the latest developments in technology by reading articles in *The Wall Street Journal* and trade publications and attending lectures at Carnegie-Mellon University in Pittsburgh. It wasn't even his field, but he was intrigued by it. He was the epitome of the lifelong learner.

When you're in the process of learning something new, it's exciting. If you are studying in a classroom or group setting, you're meeting new people and soaking up different viewpoints. That's stimulating in its own right. Your perception of the world around you changes ever so slightly, and you make connections you never made before.

Learning boosts your mood as well as your promotion prospects. "It's vital to continue to master skills and find new challenges to keep up your spirits about work," says career coach Jones. "When you're learning, you're in a different mind-set. Everything becomes heightened. It's a state of growth. It's energizing."

Another bonus is that by adding skills and stretching yourself, you're more likely to take advantage of opportunities and you won't be overly frightened to shift in a new direction in your job. Look at the great leaders: They're always adding to their knowledge, practicing new skills, and sharing this information with others, she adds.

So if you're feeling stuck in your job and don't know what to do next, charge up your brain cells. Even if you have only a hazy notion of what interests you, go to the library and take out a book or two on the subject. Enroll in just one class.

When thinking about my career, I say to myself, "I will find opportunities to learn X and gain experience in Y." With a career map in mind, you are the one behind the wheel. For most of us, career satisfaction and growth don't happen just because someone above us at work opened the door for us. It's great when that happens, but you still need the skills or leadership ability required to succeed.

Seek out openings to spread your wings, or find ways to bring more variety to your duties at work. To discover these opportunities, get a grip on how your company works, not just your department. How does it make money? Who are the key people running the show? How did those leaders get where they are? What qualities do they bring to their work? What is it about their management style that appeals to you?

Look at the job descriptions of the positions that interest you at your current employer and make note of the skills or qualifications required. Adopting a holistic approach to "learning" about your workplace can naturally give you clues to where you might find innovative projects and assignments or create one for yourself. So get curious about your company and its mission and inner workings.

Here's an idea: Play a mental game with yourself. Pretend you've just been offered your job at your firm and you want to get a feel for the culture, what the job entails, and whether you would fit it. Step back and peer in with fresh eyes from an outsider's perspective. What might you negotiate for that would make it a job you love or want to accept? It might surprise you.

Learning is a broad, sweeping adventure. It can start with simply gathering information about what things would make a job valuable to you. We started on some of this work in earlier chapters. But as you get older, learning becomes even more imperative if you want to stay relevant in the workplace and keep your ballast as new technology arrives and younger bosses step in to manage you. In truth, being open to learning new ways to improve your abilities isn't an option. No one can coast in today's job market—or in one's life outside the office either.

Learning and Healthy Aging

It's up to you to be accountable for your job. At the core, you need to trust in yourself and your abilities—especially your moxie to gain new knowledge at any age. "People rarely succeed unless they have fun in what they are doing," Dale Carnegie, author of *How to Win Friends and Influence People*, an uber-bestseller first published in 1936, once said. And to me—and to you, I hope—learning is fun, or to paraphrase an old commercial, it's *fun*damental. It gets your mind moving.

Things are changing so rapidly that being up-to-date with the latest developments in your field is more important now than ever—especially since more and more Boomers are pushing back their retirement dates. A whopping 65 percent of Baby Boomers plan to work past age 65 or have no plans to retire, and 52 percent expect to continue working, at least on a part-time basis, after they retire, according to a recent survey by Transamerica Center for Retirement Studies.

And when asked what steps they're taking to ensure that they can continue working past age 65, 41 percent of workers said they're keeping job skills up-to-date, and 11 percent are going back to school to learn new skills.

One of the classic negative stereotypes employers hold about older workers is that they're uninterested in learning new skills or incapable of doing so, or less capable than younger workers. They're somehow less trainable than younger workers, slow at processing information, resistant to new technology, and less flexible.

Such attitudes certainly don't make for an upbeat work environment. But there are things you can do.

Think Like an Entrepreneur

As I suggested earlier, one way to achieve happiness in your job is to reframe it to think like an entrepreneur. Know that you *own* your career, and that nobody else is going to chart your path. Even if you feel like a cog inside a big organization, you can run your career like a one-person business.

Think about your brand, recognize who your customers and your bosses are, and be clear about what they pay you for. Look for new ways to add value, and keep expanding the range of "products" you sell.

Ramp up your computer savvy, for instance, with a course on how to use social media tools.

Depending on your job, it might be a great move to smooth your communication skills by enrolling in a class on public speaking or joining a Toastmasters group.

You might upgrade your financial acumen by taking an accounting class. I will explore more ways to ramp up your education, and how to pay for it, in a minute.

It doesn't have to be a structured class or course per se. Skills-based learning is just one aspect of upgrading your game. I truly believe that lifelong learning is fundamental to inner happiness. There is a plethora of ways you can learn each day that may or may not change the way you approach your work life in dramatic ways but will give it meaning.

It may sound kind of "New Agey," but learning is living. Look around you every day to see what you're adding to your knowledge about the world, yourself, your work, and human relations. You never know when a new idea will spark you to make a change in your work life, to move in a new direction. You can't plan for that. Maybe it's kismet. But you have to put yourself out there to be open for it.

Give yourself permission to stretch. Ask for the hard assignments; put your hand up. Do things that make you a little uncomfortable. You'll learn from them. And you'll learn from your mistakes, too.

Stay Relevant

As author Bruce Rosenstein writes in *Create Your Future the Peter Drucker Way*, it's your responsibility to "remain relevant" in your work. Drucker, the political economist and author, who is often called the "father of modern management," once said, "Self-development may require learning new skills, new knowledge, and new manners." As Rosenstein told me, "Drucker believed that education never ended for a successful knowledge worker."

In his book, Rosenstein pointed to a commencement speech that Drucker delivered at the University of Scranton, in Pennsylvania, in 1964. "Drucker spoke that day of how people must transform their lives on an ongoing basis, as the world is continually changing, requiring different work and different knowledge as people further their lives and careers," Rosenstein writes.. "He believed that education never ended ... that creating the future required a daily, purposeful, roll-up-your-sleeves approach." Another quote from Drucker says it all: "To make the future happen requires work rather than genius."

Other big thinkers have hit a similar theme. In his insightful book *The Big Shift*, Marc Freedman firmly declares the need for ongoing adult education for all of us to remain relevant. "We are rewriting the map of life," says Freedman, CEO and founder of Encore. org, the nonprofit organization that's building a movement to tap the skills and experience of those in midlife and beyond to improve communities. "In the past, if you were 56 or 57, it might only be a year or two before you were ready to slip into early retirement," he told me. "Now, you're thinking about another 10- or 15-year working career. That changes the entire equation about what you want to do in your job, what's possible to do—and whether it's worth investing up front for additional education."

Stay Educated

In his insightful book *The Inner Game of Work*, author W. Timothy Gallwey asks: What is your definition of work? Is it all about your performance, what you *do* each day? Do you define your happiness at work by your ability to meet sales goals or bring a project in ahead of time? Is it about winning prizes?

Gallwey's theory about work is while performance is part of it, and it's great to achieve those kinds of measurable results, learning and enjoyment are just as important when it comes to loving our jobs. You're either growing, evolving, and developing your capabilities, or you're stagnating, he writes. In the worst-case scenario, you're "devolving" at work—in other words, "becoming less of yourself."

Maybe that's what's been nagging at you.

Both Gallwey and I believe, as you can tell by now, that learning is a colossal component of work and not just a by-product. Just showing up every day and getting the job done is a waste of your time. What gives your job meaning and the occasional flashes of magic is getting smarter in the process, adding value not only to your own bag of tricks but as a way to help your company achieve as well. That's what they are paying you for, after all. "You must declare yourself a *learner* during your working hours, as well as a *doer*," Gallwey writes.

I like that distinction. He's right. It's a winning combination. If you can just shake out the cobwebs, you'll discover that the desire to learn is intrinsic in all of us. Look around. There are all kinds of ways you can learn if you're open to it and willing to make a little effort. I devote a section to lifelong learning—and ways to pay for it—later in this chapter.

Hit the Road

One way I keep learning is by traveling. This is a simple way to push your mind and recharge. Travel changes us. We learn, grow, and open our minds when we leave our comfort zones, particularly if we're fortunate enough to visit a foreign country and immerse ourselves in a new culture. Try it. Changing places and routines, even for a short while, is motivating and stimulating. And when you get back to the office, it clings to you.

Your travel adventure can be informal, either on your own or with friends and family. You might even just spend one day a month walking around your own town and looking at it through the eyes of a tourist. Stop by an arboretum, tour a historical building, or visit a museum exhibit and shell out a few bucks for the guided headphone explanations of what's before your eyes.

Then, too, you might go all in and take part in a learning vacation, such as those offered by National Geographic Expeditions (nationalgeographicexpeditions.com), Road Scholar Educational Travel (roadscholar.org), Smithsonian Journey (smithsonianjourneys

---

STRATEGIC QUESTIONS TO ASK YOURSELF

- What skills can I add that will pump up my performance at work?
- Which skills can I get from work experience, and which ones will I need to hit the books for?
- Am I willing to make a hard-and-fast promise to myself to make learning and self-development part of my daily job?
- Am I willing to invest the time (and perhaps money) in myself?

.org), or your alma mater. The alumni association at Duke University, my alma mater, sponsored recent trips to Vietnam and Cambodia, and Peru, as well as the Oxford Experience, where you study for two weeks at the august University of Oxford in England via one of four noncredit enrichment courses led by Oxford tutors.

Getting Over the Hurdles

So what's holding you back? My guess is that your answer is three-fold: the cost, the lack of time, and a routine that's hard to break out of.

The second two are challenges that only you can address. It's personal. Taking classes and studying can require a significant time commitment. Taking classes and pursuing certifications means evenings and weekends, and most people are leery of adding one more thing to their to-do list.

But you can make it enjoyable. What you choose to learn about might not be directly related in an obvious way to your work. That's okay. One way to find the time and the will to shake things up is to start with baby steps, one class at a time, and that's often easier to do when it's something you're doing simply because you love it.

The money challenge is more concrete, but that can often be solved. Investigate these possibilities.

Get Someone Else to Pay

When a friend of mine, who was in a marketing position at his firm, where he had worked for 30 years, wanted to take evening classes to hone his painting technique, his employer paid the tuition. It was his hobby, but his boss agreed to support his "creative development." He justified it by recognizing that my friend managed a group of artistic designers and writers.

Roughly half of employers offer tuition assistance to employees, according to the Society for Human Resource Management. Many employers offer tax-free tuition-assistance programs—up to $5,250, not counted as taxable income—and the contribution doesn't have to be attached to a full-degree program. You may have to repay the funds, though, if you don't stay with the company for a certain number of years afterward. And you may need to earn a minimum grade or get your manager's approval for the curriculum to be eligible for this workplace perk.

Admittedly, you might need to do some smooth talking to convince your boss that your course of study will resonate, even tangentially, with your current job. But nothing ventured, nothing gained. In essence, you'll need to explain how continuing education will make you a more productive and creative worker. In other words, what's in it for the company?

Search Out Affordable Options

With or without employer assistance, paying for your career education doesn't have cut too deeply into your wallet.

Before enrolling anywhere, determine whether the program is worth the money. Keep in mind that the faster the training, the less value it may have. A certificate that you earn in a long weekend probably won't deliver the knowledge and gravitas you would get from one that requires 100 or more hours of class time at a top university. Track down graduates of programs that interest you to get a sense for how valuable it was to them. If it's related directly to learning new job skills, ask your boss for his or her opinion.

Here are some suggestions on how to save money on tuition, whether you want to get an undergraduate or graduate degree, a certificate, or just enroll in a few college courses.

- *Listen to a lecture.* Sit in on a lecture at a community center or library, or sign up for a series. Get your hands dirty in a workshop, or watch an educational video on a subject that interests you. You'll find a variety of informal learning selections at online educational sites like the Khan Academy (khanacademy.org) and TED (ted.com) videos.
- *Sign up for a MOOC online course.* MOOC is the acronym for the trendy massively open online courses, offered by companies like Coursera (coursera.org), EdX (edx.org), Lynda (lynda.com), and Udacity (udacity.com). Search for "free online courses" on The Mind Unleashed web site (themindunleashed.org) for more.

  I recently signed up for another free 12-week course called "Think Again: How to Reason and Argue," via Coursera. The class is taught by two professors at Duke University, and each week will be divided into multiple video segments that can be grouped as three lectures or viewed separately. There will be short exercises after each segment (to check comprehension) and several longer midterm quizzes. All I need for the class is a working computer and an Internet connection. Otherwise, it's free. But the course description does say it will require five or six hours of work a week.

Offered by top-tier universities like Stanford and Princeton, MOOCs offer cheap ways to learn from their instructors anytime, anywhere. And yes, if I successfully complete the class, I will receive a "Statement of Accomplishment" signed by the instructor. Of course, I'll add that to my LinkedIn profile and let my bosses know I passed with flying colors. Maybe I will show them what I learned firsthand.

- *Check out other free course options.* You may be able to audit or take free-or low-cost courses at your alma mater, or find an Osher Learning Center (usm.maine.edu/olli/national/) course being offered near you, or a noncredit personal enrichment program, such as Odyssey (advanced.jhu.ed), offered by Johns Hopkins University. Odyssey has a wide selection of courses, workshops, and lecture series delivered by faculty and community experts. Odyssey doesn't have grades or exams.

- *Take a class at a community college.* If you can't travel to a foreign country or a new city, take a class on a topic that interests you. You can start with just one course at a time at a local college, university, or community college.

  Especially worth checking out: the American Association of Community Colleges' Plus 50 Initiative at 18 schools across the country, whose curriculum is designed to help students 50 and older. The number of students ages 50 to 64 has been climbing steadily. To meet the demand for continuing education, colleges are creating retraining and certificate programs aimed squarely at this demographic.

  Community college courses are usually a few hundred dollars per credit. Online webinars and workshops offered by industry associations are other avenues to consider.

- *Try a certificate program.* Compared to full-blown degree programs, certificate programs are generally cheaper and more focused on the professional skills you may want to add now. A certificate program might run the gamut from $3,000 if done entirely online to $15,000 for on-campus credit hours. That can be quite a bit cheaper than a public four-year college degree program, which can cost you upwards of $650 per credit, or a single course at a private college, which can top $1,300. A master's degree can easily set you back more than $40,000, depending on the school.

- *Look for free or discounted tuition based on your age.* A growing number of colleges cut tuition for students 60 or older. California's 23 state universities offer free tuition in their Over 60 Program, for example, and all of Texas' public colleges and universities have tuition reduction programs for students 55 or older. Check with your state's department of education to see if there are similar deals near you.

- *Negotiate for an accelerated degree.* If you're planning for a degree, you may be able to get your tuition lowered by getting the college to waive some required courses because of your "experiential" credit. You might have a strong case that you've learned through work and life what the courses teach. Don't be bashful about advocating for yourself.

- *Get Uncle Sam to share your tuition costs.* There is a mixture of education tax breaks. To see whether you'd qualify for any of these credits or deductions, visit the Tax Benefits for Education Information Center on the IRS web site (irs.gov) and IRS Publication 970: Tax Benefits for Education.

  The Lifetime Learning Credit, for example, can give you a tax credit of up to $2,000 to cover up to 20 percent of annual tuition; you don't have to be enrolled in a degree program. (The benefit phases out completely for married couples earning $124,000 and singles earning $62,000.)

  You might consider a low-interest federal Stafford Loan— there's no age limit, and you're eligible as a part-time student, too. Go to FinAid.org and Edvisors.com for information on scholarships and grants for older students.

- *For an undergraduate degree, check out federal Pell grants.* They're interest-free and don't need to be repaid; the most recent maximum award is $5,730.

The amount you'll qualify for depends on factors such as your financial need, tuition costs, and whether you'll be a full-time or part-time student. For more on this type of aid, go to the Pell grant area of the U.S. Department of Education's web site.

- *Save through a 529 plan.* This tax-favored program, run by the states, isn't just for your child's or grandchild's college tuition. People of any age can invest money in a 529 plan and use the cash for their future education costs. A 529's earnings are tax free when you withdraw the money to pay higher education expenses. Some states even let residents deduct 529 contributions from their state income taxes. And if you wind up not using some or all of the money, you can transfer the funds to another beneficiary, like your child or grandchild. You can research 529 plans at Savingforcollege.com or the web site of the College Savings Plans Network.

- *Try to score an older-student grant, scholarship, or fellowship.* Some groups and foundations offer them, though it may take some investigating to track down this interest-free financing. The American Association of University Women, for example, offers fellowships and grants for women going back to school to advance their careers, change careers, or reenter the workforce. For more on grants, scholarships, and fellowships, check out the sites FastWeb.com and FinAid.org.

- *If you must borrow, be conservative.* The Consumer Financial Protection Bureau (consumerfinance.gov) site has excellent college financing advice to help you choose the right loan and pay the least amount of interest. Try to get a Federal Direct Loan. Rates on these loans are fixed and low.

  You may be able to get your monthly student loan payments reduced if you work in public safety, public health, education, social work, or the nonprofit sector. Learn more at the Public Service Loan Forgiveness Program area of the Department of Education site (studentaid.ed.gov).

Take an Educational Sabbatical

Some employers offer paid time-out breaks, or sabbaticals, of up to six months that can allow you to work with a charity, take an immersion program in a foreign language, or do something you've been dreaming of doing. If you can swing it, this kind of escape clause can do wonders for your attitude and builds a feeling of goodwill toward your employer, which can have long-lasting effects for both you and for your company.

That said, the benefit isn't widely available. According to a 2014 study of employee benefits conducted by the Society for Human Resource Management, 5 percent of the 500 or so companies surveyed offered paid sabbatical programs in 2009. That dropped to 4 percent in 2013. Unpaid sabbatical leave, however, grew to 16 percent from 12 percent during the period. Sabbaticals are generally available to employees after at least five years, according to Pat Katepoo, founder of WorkOptions, a firm that helps employees negotiate for flexible work time.

Even if your employer doesn't have a formal program for long-term employees, there's no harm in asking—provided that you have a well-thought-out plan for how you'll spend the time. It helps if you can make an argument for how your plans will benefit your employer at some stage. Remember that whenever you're negotiating for changes with your employer, from flextime to accepting a short-term assignment in another department to a sabbatical, you *always* need to think of it from the perspective of your manager—what's in it for him or her—and for the company overall.

The snag is that taking a chunk of time off can be difficult to do. That's mostly because you're afraid of the "out of sight, out of mind" repercussions that time away from the office might have on your job security down the road. You worry that the time away from the office will probably kill any chances for a raise and push you out of contention for promotion in the near future. And you fear that it may reveal that you're somehow not an "essential" worker and that your company can get by just fine without you.

Meanwhile, taking time off might hit your pocketbook, too, if the sabbatical is unpaid, so you'll need to have savings set aside to cover your expenses. You can probably negotiate using your existing vacation and leave pay to cover a portion of it, but expect to negotiate for whether or not you need to pay for your own health benefits while you're gone.

Then, too, you may have to agree to stay in your job for a certain period of time when you return or you'll have to pay back any salary you received during your sabbatical. Employers worry that you might be using the sabbatical as a segue to ultimately leaving. If you're a valued employee, they don't want to risk losing you—whether or not they think you're happy on the job.

It's a good idea to start thinking about taking a sabbatical at least a year ahead of time. Generally speaking, a well-thought-out sabbatical entails lots of research. But if you have a rational plan, your employer may be willing to green-light it, particularly if there's an upside for the firm somewhere down the line.

That said, I'd advise asking for a mini-sabbatical—a month or two tops. Six weeks is typically a realistic period because it gives you plenty of time to travel or throw yourself into a program of some sort, plus breathing room for reentry to the office again when you get back.

Ed Redfern, one of my colleagues at AARP, for example, practices Ashtanga yoga daily in Washington, D.C. In 2013, because he'd worked at AARP for more than seven years, he was able to take advantage of the company's "renewal program." Ed spent six weeks immersed in his yoga practice in India, under the instruction of Sharath Jois at the K. Pattabhi Jois Ashtanga Yoga Institute in Mysore, India. For Ed, it was a game-changer.

"The renewal accelerated my practice," he says. He also returned to the office refocused, energized, and eager to get back to work. "The transforming effects made me eager to continue working toward my life's purpose—to help others live their true purpose in life and experience being alive as spiritual/emotional beings—which my work enables," he told me.

Interested? Here's your action plan. First, check with your human resources department to see if your company has a sabbatical program. If not and you're thinking of designing your own, you'll need to figure out how you want to negotiate for one. This will depend largely on whether or not you have a solid working relationship with your boss, one based firmly on respect and trust. Do you telecommute, for example, from time to time? Is time away from the office to take your mom or dad to a doctor's appointment easy to get approved? In the end, your chances of scoring a sabbatical come down to how supportive your boss is of you.

To help you plan your break, you might look into outfits such as YourSabbatical.com, which helps companies and individuals set up sabbatical programs.

When approaching your employer, your proposal should answer these three basic questions. What's your purpose? How might it benefit your employer? Who is going to do your work while you're gone? And don't feel that your sabbatical has to achieve something concrete. Just having a respite from work can give you a sense of well-being and certainly reduces stress and burnout. But you will have to know how to spin it to a higher purpose to sell your boss on your proposal.

Remember: Timing is everything. Pick your moment not only for "the ask," but also for the time of year you want to be absent. You want to be sure that it's not a busy time of year for your employer's business.

Parting thought: B. C. Forbes, the founder and first publisher of *Forbes* magazine, once said: "Think not of yourself as the architect of your career but as the sculptor. Expect to have to do a lot of hard hammering and chiseling and scraping and polishing."

Chapter Recap

In this chapter, we reviewed different ways to upgrade your game—and how to afford them. We discussed the ways learning can boost your attitude and spark ideas that will reenergize your job and your overall attitude toward your work. You also learned the importance of education in ramping up your knowhow about the technology in your field, keeping up with changes and combating ageism in the workplace. Learning new skills can also help lead to new responsibilities at work and make you more valuable to your employer. Generally speaking, that feels good from an ego perspective. Taking the time to learn and grow through travel or a sabbatical away from the office can also be the panacea you need to reboot.

Your To-Do List

- In your Job Remodeling journal, note the activities that keep you fresh and learning.
- Write down the activities you take part in that involve learning in some fashion.
- Jot down in your journal what your favorite classes were in grade school, high school, and college, and why.

- Write down in your journal a list of skills you could add that would make you more valuable to your boss or position you to take on projects that would challenge you.
- Jot down in your journal several subjects you've always wanted to learn more about but haven't had time.
- Create a blueprint for workshops, classes, or certificates or degrees you would need to love your job or even move into your dream job at your current employer.
- Start researching where you might study, how much time you can realistically commit, and your options for paying the tab.
- Pick one class to get started, even if it's just for fun. You never know where it might lead.
- If a sabbatical is feasible, think about whether it might give you the time to refresh your workplace skills and attitude.

8

How to Have the "What's Next?" Talk with Your Boss

■ ■ ■

Sooner or later you'll have to suck it up and have the "talk" with your boss. Don't roll your eyes. You can do this. Stop dawdling.

It's unlikely that you will simply be handed a new opportunity, or a bump in salary, on a silver platter without asking. "Speak now or forever hold your peace," as my father used to say to me when it was time to make a choice or decision. This chapter will show you how to speak now, and how to have that critical conversation you've been having in your own head for so long.

The time has come to channel your inner salesperson. "Like it or not, we are all in sales," Daniel Pink, bestselling author of *To Sell Is Human: The Surprising Truth about Moving Others,* told me. He explained to me, as he does in his book, that in his mind, "every person in the world is now engaged in sales. It's not about going door-to-door selling products, but about moving people, convincing them to go along with your idea, your project."

To find a solution to your job blues, you either have to tough it out and pretend all is well until you can make those internal changes we discussed earlier, or find a way to persuade your boss to make some changes in your situation. Think Sales 101. One of the best ways to get your mental game ready for this conversation is to step into your boss's shoes, metaphorically speaking.

"To be great at sales, you need to be able to get out of your own mind to see from another's point of view," Pink says. Ask yourself, "What's in it for him or her?" And you need to be careful not to push too hard to force a quick decision.

If you've made it to this final chapter, you've spent quite a bit of time figuring out what kinds of changes in your job and in yourself will help you jump-start your attitude and your work life. You've completed a deep assessment of who you are, and you've set goals you want to achieve—both short-term and long-term. But the needle won't move until you take action to make the change a reality and set your plan in motion.

Nine times out of ten, this means you'll have to have a face-to-face, sit-down conversation with your boss or supervisor to ask for help. These can be small adjustments to your work schedule, far-reaching moves to different work in another part of the company, the resources needed to take a class, or an increase in salary commensurate with your commitment and sense of self-worth. Are you ready?

The Time Is Now

No matter what you want out of that upcoming talk with the boss, you couldn't choose a better time to ask. An increasing number of companies worldwide are getting the message that their employees aren't happy about going to work each day because they aren't challenged or feeling appreciated. A study by Harris Interactive showed that two out of three people would consider leaving their jobs right now if they could. So what's new? Plenty. The tide is turning when it comes to the employer-employee dynamic, so this could be a very good time to step forward with your request.

As I am writing this, the economy continues to strengthen, and employee turnover is already on the rise, according to workplace experts I've interviewed. As a result, companies are starting to dance a bit to keep their employees involved and happy in their jobs. For the first time in years, employers are actually a little scared about losing good workers. Managers know full well that any lingering discontent from the past few years of belt-tightening, paltry raises or none at all, and ongoing cutbacks may result in "adios, amigo," as skilled employees head on to greener pastures.

And it's not just in the United States. Companies around the globe are grappling with talent shortages and scrambling to snatch the best and brightest from the workforce, according to Matt Grunewald, a research consultant at LinkedIn. "In their hunt for great hires, though, companies are failing to retain their own high performers, which is costing them big," he says.

LinkedIn surveyed more than 7,500 members across the United States, Australia, Canada, India, and the United Kingdom, who recently changed jobs. Sixty-eight percent of survey respondents in the United States said it was actually easier to find an open position *outside* of their company than within it, according to LinkedIn's 2014 "Employees Overboard" report. "Tempted by the prospect of landing a better gig, more and more employees are weighing their options. Fully 85 percent of the workforce is either actively looking for a job or open to talking to recruiters about relevant opportunities, up from 80 percent in 2012," says Grunewald.

As a result, many firms realize that they must find new ways to hang on to talented employees for as long as they can. They're desperately seeking … well, loyalty.

The larger issue, however, may be that employee discontent is hitting employers where it hurts—on the bottom line. It's expensive to replace you, and fewer workers are coming up behind you to fill slots that demand experience. Then, too, Millennials tend to switch jobs more frequently than Boomers, so employers really do have an incentive to keep you happy and showing up each day because you *want* to, not because you *need* to.

So as you go into the talk, boost your confidence by keeping this in mind: Your boss needs you.

Depending on your position and industry, the total cost of replacing you can range from thousands of dollars to as much as one-and-a-half times your annual salary. This cost includes the fees that go hand-in-hand with recruiting and advertising your job, the time and money spent bringing someone in for an interview, and the cost of training someone. Plus, there's the loss of institutional knowledge that goes out the door with you—hard to put a price on. Now tack on the stress your manager and coworkers must shoulder to make up for the work that falls between the cracks when you leave. And, finally, toss in the potential toll the loss of a terrific team member can take on the morale of those left behind. Now your employer has a serious problem.

To be honest, most workers I talk to don't really want to leave their jobs. Sure, they complain a lot, but when pressed, they say they like their coworkers, and they don't want the hassle and stress of changing jobs. In fact, they dread the thought of being the new kid on the block somewhere else. They *do*, however, want to enjoy what they're doing *right now*, to be paid a fair salary for it, and to know they aren't stuck there in that particular job or assignment for too long. Maybe it's our increasingly short attention spans, but "nimble" is in. Even if they can't be promoted per se, they want to keep getting better at what they do, and be rewarded in some way for doing it.

Questions to Ask Yourself before the Big Meeting

It's time to begin thinking about how to make the move. Let's start with several questions to consider before you have that talk with your boss.

- *Are you sold on what you're asking for?* In other words, have you convinced yourself? Is the change you're seeking going to make your job better in some way or your life richer? You can sell it only if you yourself are persuaded. So consider—why you? Why now?
- *What exactly are you asking for?* Can you say it in a sentence? Do you have a well-defined proposal? You need to be able to cut to the chase quickly, and explain what it is you're asking for. Your pitch must be clear, simply stated, and delivered without setting the stage with a lot of preamble and throat-clearing.
- *What are your boss's challenges right now?* Does he or she work for a difficult boss? Is your department in the midst of cutbacks? Does your boss love her job? Take the time to do your research to get a feel for what your boss faces before you go for the "ask." This mind-set will allow you to anticipate potential push-back that might stem from her different vantage point. When you understand where somebody's coming from, you can do a much better job of anticipating problems and responding to her worries.

- *Can you think of anything funny to say?* In some circumstances, a joke can be a great way to get the conversation started. Not all of us can do this, but if it's in your wheelhouse, you might tastefully pull it off. Don't make it a self-deprecating joke, though. This is not the time to cast yourself in a "less than" light. Depending on your boss, this approach can ease the up-front tension of your "ask."

- *Do you have a whistle-stopping presentation?* Can you do it in your sleep? Practice *does* make perfect, so spend as much time as you need to get it down to a convincing "conversation" that you allows you to smoothly deliver your well-thought-out pitch. Envision the presentation as a poised, relaxed, well-rehearsed soft-shoe dance. It should appear effortless, but at its core it is the end result of days of practice and preparation.

- *Are you genuinely passionate about what you're asking for?* The kind of energy and enthusiasm that you exude when you're passionate about something can light up a room. It's contagious.

- *Are you comfortable saying, "I don't know"?* It's better to admit ignorance than to take a stab at answering a tough question your boss may lob your way when you ask for a promotion, a raise, a move to a new position, a sabbatical, what have you. It's better to admit you don't have the answer but will get back to him than to avoid it all together or wing it.

- *How quickly do you realistically want, or need, something to happen?* Can you wait a while to let it all fall into place? The earlier you can start a conversation about a change you would like to make in your work, the better your chances of getting the result you're after. If your boss is not under time pressure to meet sales goals or turn a project around for higher-ups, and you aren't either, it's far easier to work toward a solution together as a team.

- *Is your boss really your adversary?* Or is it just convenient to portray her as the bad cop to keep you off the hook from taking charge of your work life? Most of the time he or she truly wants you to succeed, to be happy and engaged in your work. After all, it's ultimately a reflection on her and her management acumen.

Your Plan-and-Prepare Strategy

Consider these six steps before you talk to your boss.

Step 1: What's in It for Them?

To reiterate, your core strategy is to pitch your boss on your dream assignment, promotion, flexible schedule, professional development class, or mentor opportunity using Daniel Pink's "what's in it for them" approach. Ask yourself:

- How can the company benefit from helping you do something different?
- How can your boss professionally win from it?
- Is it going to cost your company anything in terms of money, time, or personnel changes?

It's not about what your "ask" can do for you. It's about what your "ask" can do for them. Never forget that. Build your pitch by first thinking of it from your boss's perspective.

If you move to another department, for example, will that just create a problem for him? Will your boss have to find someone to replace you? Even if it's just a temporary assignment to help out in another department when someone goes on maternity leave, it still can be one more thing to deal with from a management perspective. Your job still needs to get done. It might even cost money from your boss's departmental budget to hire a temporary contract worker to do your job in the interim.

Plus, some especially paranoid bosses might interpret your aspiration to tackle a new assignment outside of your department, even for a few months, as a sign that you're unhappy working for them. So you may need to put on those kid gloves. A good understanding of your boss's personality and what motivates her will help you devise your best approach. This can take some keen observation ahead of time to avoid having the wheels come off the conversation from the get-go.

So think strategically and build your case by explaining clearly how your boss and your department can benefit, and do everything you can to make the transition easy for them.

Step 2: Play Your Cards Close to the Vest

Regardless of what you're looking to change, whether it's asking for a promotion or upgrading your game with a sabbatical, stay cool.

If, for example, it's a lateral move to another position or department within the company you're after, keep your hunt on the Q-T until you know what possible opportunities there might be for you. To get some idea of available openings, check out your company's internal web site to see what jobs are currently posted.

Which ones intrigue you? Hunt through all the nooks and crannies of the various departments with a fine-tooth comb. Look for jobs that hold out the promise of sparking your creativity.

Talk to coworkers about their positions and what they love about what they do. These kinds of informal discussions can be inspiring and can trigger ideas for how you might be able to transition to something new.

If a job opening has already been listed to the outside world, check out your company on LinkedIn, and you can probably find out more about the particulars. It's best, of course, to learn about an opportunity before it gets announced to the outside world.

Step 3: Talk to Colleagues Who Have Made Similar Changes

If you handle these conversations gracefully, you can find out lots of information. Was their boss supportive? Did the HR department help pilot the change?

If you're asking for a flexible schedule, for example, talk to others who have similar schedules and find out about company policies. If you are seeking out a position in another department, check to see if your company has an in-house referral site. If you know someone who knows your work and can refer you to an open position in the area, ask him or her about it. Some companies offer cash bonuses to employees who refer others in the firm to open positions, should that person get the position. The referring employee also benefits from getting to work with someone they know and like. It's simple human nature. Managers are more willing to consider someone who has been given the thumbs-up by someone they know and trust within the organization. So internal introductions can definitely help open pathways for you.

Step 4: Tweak Your Elevator Speech

Practice explaining what it is that's pushing you to want to take this step. What are your goals? Why are you best suited for this? Can you show how the new duties will ramp up your skills and make you a more valuable employee in a concrete way? Or demonstrate how the company will gain by allowing you to tap into your existing skills in ways that you haven't been able to showcase in your current position?

Step 5. Schedule a Formal Meeting with Your Boss

Don't wing this meeting. Make a formal presentation, with all of the necessary bells and whistles. When the time arrives, pay attention to your posture. When we're anxious, we tend to collapse our chests and fidget in our chairs. Make eye contact and be sure to smile. Explain why and how you'll be a star in the position you're aiming for, or why everyone will benefit from your upgrading your game.

And give the boss time to consider your request and to get back to you. Avoid demands and "I need to know right now" pressure sales. He may have to get permission from his boss or just get comfortable with the changes you asked for.

A man in his 50s who works in marketing at a large company called me recently for some advice. He had asked his immediate boss if he could possibly step into a temporary opening in another department for a few months, an assignment that would involve using his marketing skills, but with a different product. The short-term gig to cover for someone going on a medical leave, he explained, would help him learn more about another part of the company and build synergies.

"It didn't go as I expected," he told me. "It definitely didn't go the way I wanted it to."

What happened? His boss thought that because he was asking to shift assignments, he was unhappy. And if someone else could so easily jump in to do the job for a few months, then why did they need him at all?

Gulp. Nope. Not the way he wanted that conversation to go.

Step 6: Make Some Noise

There's a reason why you're stuck. You've been living under the false impression that laying low and under the radar might keep you out of the firing line. If you're miserable, cut it out. It's time to be heard.

Many people feel awkward with the bragging that comes along with asking for a new job, a change in responsibilities, a raise. I get it. So turn it around—approach these conversations as if you are just voicing an "interest in" or starting a "discussion" about innovative ways you can contribute to the company.

What do you have to lose? Your supervisor can always say no, and you're right where you are now. But if you say nothing, management will never know that you're ready to take on different duties or learn something new, or even that you're unhappy where you are.

If you're like me, the whole notion of meeting with your boss to talk about what's ahead is daunting, and more than a little nerve-wracking. But if you want to make a move, no matter what kind, say something. Your mental health depends on it.

The discussion doesn't have to be prickly. Your boss is probably oblivious to the fact that you're discouraged. So sit up straight and get your mojo going. This is your time to highlight your ability, skills, and objectives.

In the early chapters and in your journal, you've already worked through the soul-searching required to think about what you want. You already have a handle on what your pluses are and what more you hope to be able to bring to your job in the future. You might have even added new skills, as we discussed in Chapter 7, to qualify you to make a jump.

Be clear about what you offer your company and what you're asking. There's very little risk—and tremendous reward—in asking for a stretch or a new challenge (even taking on a mentor or asking to mentor someone) if you have the talent to do it and believe in yourself. But you'll never be considered for it if you don't have that conversation—or several conversations, if that's what it takes.

Are you ready?

Carrying Out the "Ask"

Now let's talk about some specific questions and challenges that might come up in your discussion. These discussions can be fraught with nerves and overthinking, but at some stage, you just have to move the chess piece. Here goes.

The Dreaded Salary Discussion

If it's a raise you want, be clear about what you want and be ready to show why you deserve more money. The aim is for your boss to notice and recognize that you're worth more than you were last year, or even last month, and to find a way for your salary to reflect that.

Okay, I admit I said earlier that money isn't the be-all and end-all when it comes to job joy, but there is plenty to be said for being compensated fairly. I know firsthand how hard it is to find the courage to request a bump in pay. I've been there, and it hasn't always gone precisely as I'd hoped. One time I had to prove myself for another two months by writing a minimum of five feature articles for the magazine before my raise was approved.

You have to steel yourself for not getting what you want. Back to my favorite expression—"nothing ventured, nothing gained." That said, "I've never heard of anyone getting fired for asking for a raise," says career coach Phyllis Mufson.

Average hourly earnings in the United States rose a tiny 2.1 percent from 2013 to 2014, according to the Bureau of Labor Statistics. Yet top executives who changed jobs in 2013 averaged a 17 percent pay increase, according to the executive search firm Salveson Stetson Group, based in Radnor, Pennsylvania—far above the 11 percent increase in 2008 and 2009. These figures include base salary, bonus, and any signing bonus.

To me, this says that at many companies the funds are available—if you can prove your value. The task is to get those raises once you're on the payroll.

It takes spunk and mettle, but you can do it … with the proper preparation.

Women have the toughest time asking for more money. Many workplace experts say women don't push as hard for raises as men do. They're afraid of coming off as being too aggressive, and they worry about the backlash from that perception. Not surprisingly, men are four times more likely than women to ask for a salary increase, according to economist Linda Babcock of Carnegie Mellon University. And a LinkedIn survey of more than 2,000 professionals globally who are LinkedIn members found that 37 percent of men say they feel confident in career negotiations, including asking for a raise, compared with just 26 percent of women. (That said, 84 percent of women who asked for a raise last year received one, according to the survey.)

Negotiating is something many of us sweat, to be honest. Globally, 35 percent of people surveyed by LinkedIn reported feeling anxious or frightened about negotiating. Thirty-four percent felt confident, while 10 percent said negotiations were exciting, and 10 percent were indifferent about them.

A study in the journal *Organization Science* called "Engendering Inequity? How Social Accounts Create, versus Merely Explain, Unfavorable Pay Outcomes for Women" found that women received smaller raises than men did because their managers thought modest pay increases wouldn't upset women as much as their male colleagues. No kidding.

Gender issues aside, I always tell job seekers that the time to negotiate salary is when they're getting hired. Forget all the lip service you'll probably hear about raises that will likely come your way after your first glowing performance review.

Imagine that two people receive a job offer of $45,000. One negotiates for $5,000 more, a 1 percent raise yearly and a 4 percent raise every third year, but the other accepts the offer without negotiating and sees only a 1 percent pay increase each year. Even without accounting for bonuses and big promotions, after a 45-year career, the difference in the their lifetime earnings is a stunning $1,037,773, according to Salary.com.

Despite the fact that they are leaving more than $1 million on the table, a CareerBuilder survey found that nearly half of workers don't negotiate their first job offers, and two in five workers don't negotiate in their current jobs.

For most of us, raises really amount to nickels and dimes thereafter, unless you can unabashedly toot your own horn *and* have the chops to prove you're worth the extra salary. But don't lose heart—it may be harder, but it's never too late to go after more money, if that's what it will take to make you happier at work.

Waiting to ask for a raise at your annual review is usually too late, says Suzanne Lucas, who blogs as the Evil HR Lady. "You've missed the boat," she says. "The money for the year has already been allotted and your boss cannot increase your pay without taking away from your coworkers—and that isn't going to happen."

Instead, ask for a raise three to four months before your annual review, Lucas suggests. Or ask for one after you've finished a major project or fixed a tricky problem with a client. Take advantage of those signature moments before your work is forgotten.

Some big no-nos: If you haven't been in the position for at least a year, don't go asking for a raise by suggesting that you're underpaid. And never tell your boss you need a raise because you can't pay your bills, your adult children just moved back in, or your husband left you. "Your boss doesn't care. Your salary isn't determined by how much you need to spend, but by how much value you bring to the company," Lucas says. "If you're going to ask for a raise, show that you're awesome."

And don't expect that your boss will necessarily notice all your hard work and reward you. These days, budgets are cut to the bone. Instead, show her why you're due a decent increase. It helps if you've just won some sort of recognition, as Lucas says, or taken on extra duties successfully. Providing evidence of your value to your employer can pay off in your future paychecks.

That means making a list of your job responsibilities and how you've contributed to the company's bottom line. Print out all those "great job!" e-mails, letters, and other documents from clients, coworkers, and others praising your work.

Look for weaknesses in your work or places where your boss might question you in terms of your achievements. Be honest with yourself. Was there an example where you didn't make the right decision or a project wasn't well received? Have an answer ready to rebut those critiques.

Check out web sites such as glassdoor.com, payscale.com, and salary.com, for national averages and pay ranges in your industry, city, and region to get the lay of the land. Then, dig a little deeper, if possible, to get a sense of pay ranges from recruiters and people you know with similar jobs, if you can get them to spill the beans. Federal workers and applicants can easily find U.S. government salaries around the country at the web site of the U.S. Office of Personnel Management. If you work at a nonprofit, check out the organization's latest online tax filing (Form 990) to see how much its key executives and employees earn.

Don't be wishy-washy. This is your time to be pushy. So turn up the volume. Ask for more than you think you deserve in terms of the job and salary level. If you can prove you're worth it, then you *are* worth it, and your boss is likely to welcome the chance to reward you.

Have a figure in mind, but don't ask for a specific number: Suggest a range instead.

Don't take no for an answer. When you're in a pay negotiation, "get comfortable drawing out the conversation, or even postponing it, rather than nodding your head in agreement or surrendering with 'Okay,'" says Selena Rezvani, author of *Pushback: How Smart Women Ask—and Stand Up—for What They Want*. "Experiment with being silent for a few seconds to level the power and ask questions that open up dialogue."

And don't get too greedy with your must-have salary increase. Most employers typically plan for annual upticks of 5 percent or less, so ramping up to a bump of 10 percent or more is highly unlikely. But if you're also asking for a promotion, then that 10 percent may have some merit.

Either way, prepare for the meeting with a target amount in mind. I would advise that you approach your request in a direct, practical fashion. Say something like, "I'm committed and passionate about the work I do here, and I see myself working here for years to come. Based on my research of the current job market, however, I should be making X."

Whatever you do, don't make the request an ultimatum, and be cautious about accepting a counteroffer from your boss if it feels like he's throwing you a bone to keep you from flying the coop. Counteroffers can leave both of you resentful and create an uncomfortable work atmosphere. You didn't really get what you wanted and your boss felt pressured to cough up some money he hadn't budgeted for.

One caveat: If your company is laying people off and reducing costs, you might have to cool your heels until things improve. In this scenario, you might want a Plan B. If a raise is out of the question right now, your boss might have an easier time offering you a one-time bonus or stock options to show his or her appreciation for your contributions. Or she may give you a few extra personal days or comp time for some long hours you've put in on a project. You might even be able to negotiate for more vacation time.

Making Your Job Flexible—and Life Manageable

"Improved efficiency" should be at the top of your "why you should let me have a flexible work schedule or telecommute" list. Increased productivity was, in fact, one of the leading reasons for allowing employees to work from home, according to both the Challenger and Korn/Ferry surveys.

Walk into the conversation with a proposal that describes what your work schedule would be, the number of hours you would work, how unplanned overtime would be handled, how often you would check in with an office visit, and how often you would talk with your boss. You might agree to work in the office when projects are being launched or problems arise that the company needs to solve. To seal the deal, ask for a trial period of three to six months so both you and your boss can see how the arrangement works out and fine-tune it if needed.

"If you're exploring ways to take control of your working hours, keep in mind that employers are more willing to let you shuffle what you do over the course of a day, but they are more reluctant to grant you days when you are just not there or are working part-time," said Kenneth Matos, senior director of employment research and practice at the Families and Work Institute, a research group.

In the end, the best way to convince your boss is to show, not tell. That means that when you walk in for the ask, a solid work ethic that delivers reliable results will be your ticket to flex-work gold stars and, ultimately, your job happiness.

And remember: Whatever agreement you come to may not survive a new boss or job role. You may need to ask again if things change at the office.

Moving Internally

The delayed gratification of paying our dues and clawing slowly inch-by-inch up the corporate ladder is increasingly passé. That's particularly true when you've already been slogging it out for two decades. Our passion for our work is what drives us, along with our internal urge to keep developing our knowledge and talents.

Employers I've talked to are scrambling to solve the puzzle of how they can harness your passion and curiosity to their advantage. As you will see in the sidebar on Michelin North America, the best employers have already moved away from the old-school model of plugging people into preset job descriptions and categories. Instead, they're coming up with innovative ways to work with their employees, like you, to become a "partner" on your career path moving forward. But it's up to you to make the new paradigm work.

Offering employees the opportunities to have the flexibility and mobility to take on new responsibilities, to shift between jobs in a company, to work abroad, and more, is increasingly critical to retaining employees. According to LinkedIn's "Employees Overboard" survey, members from around the world who had recently left their jobs were asked why they jumped ship. The number one reason: They were looking for a greater opportunity for advancement. That desire was followed by a search for better leadership, and then a bump in compensation and benefits.

If you've been in your position for a while and have taken on extra responsibilities over time, ask about a promotion. Or consider a title change or revision to your job description, which may help get you the recognition and respect you've wanted. A more prestigious title has a future payoff, especially if you decide to switch jobs down the road. A prospective employer will be impressed by it, and you may have an easier time landing a higher salary.

If you can't move up, offer to work on something that is not part of your day-to-day responsibilities. Is there a special company initiative or a project no one wants to take on? Perhaps there's a job-share available that would allow you to work for another department for a few months, as I discussed previously. If there's an employee out on leave, maybe you can fill that job in the interim.

Explain how your new responsibilities will help the company. Perhaps you'll be able to bring a fresh perspective, produce creative ideas, or provide experienced leadership to a particular project.

Opportunities for internal mobility are key to retaining employees, according to LinkedIn's research. At U.S. companies, 38 percent of employees who made internal moves would have left had they not been able to do so. The figures in other countries are similar: in Australia, it's 49 percent; Canada, 44; India, 43; and the United Kingdom, 45.

"People need to know that their career development and growth are valued as much as, if not more than, hiring external people," says Phil Hendrickson, manager of global talent sourcing strategy at Starbucks. "You solve three things at once when you hire someone internally: You fill a role, you retain a good employee, and you improve your talent brand."

My point is that at the heart of it, job happiness is truly a two-way street. Employers want you to be happy as much as you want to be. This sounds counterintuitive, given the old business model we all grew up with. But I see these changes happening in the workplace at large employers as well as small start-ups. So before you get yourself in knots about how to ask for a change in your job, do some additional homework to see if there is already a structure in place that will help you do just that.

According to LinkedIn's 2013 Global Recruiting Trends Survey of almost 3,400 human resource and talent acquisition professionals in 19 countries, about two-thirds of companies in the United States, Canada, India, Australia, and the United Kingdom say they already have a formal internal mobility program.

But I don't think many employees know about these efforts. Employers need to do a better job of letting them know. They shouldn't "underestimate the power of internal and external distribution channels—like newsletters, the company intranet, company all-hands meetings, LinkedIn, Twitter, and Facebook—to publicize stories of employees who have moved around in the organization," says Dr. Robin Erickson, who directs Bersin by Deloitte's Talent Acquisition research practice.

So as you prepare to talk to your boss about your bid for a change, keep in mind that she, too, may be trying to grasp what motivates you, what your career goals are, and what kinds of opportunities she can provide that will help you both succeed. Then, too, she may be getting pressure from above to retain you. Until you have that conversation, she may very well be in the dark about what kinds of things she can offer that will click.

Upgrading Your Game

If you're interested in continuing your education, ask your boss if she would support your desire to take a workshop or go back to school for a certification or an advanced degree. See if she would be willing to give you some flextime to help you fit your studies into your schedule. As I discussed in the Chapter 7, check and see if your employer can help pay some of your tuition.

Another way to ramp up your inner game is to seek out a mentor or sponsor. Many big corporations offer sponsorship and mentoring programs. If yours doesn't have a formal mentoring arrangement, let your boss know that you're interested in being connected with someone senior or with more experience. Many coworkers are eager to lend a hand. It's flattering and empowering to have the experience and gravitas needed to help a less experienced colleague. Roberta Terkowitz, for example, says mentoring her IBM coworkers gave *her* fresh joy in her job. "I enjoyed helping others succeed, particularly when they were new to a job," Terkowitz told me. "I felt like I was making a contribution, and that got me out of bed in the morning."

A CONVERSATION WITH MICHELIN'S HERB JOHNSON

Herb Johnson, 61, has spent his entire professional life in the tire industry, logging more than three decades at Michelin, where he was a former director of the brand's motorsports division and director of community relations. Now he's the chief diversity officer, responsible for making the firm's internal employee relations stronger, building loyalty, and motivating employees to be part of the company's mission.

"This is what I call a dream assignment, my capstone assignment. I'm in the giving-back stage of my career," says Johnson, who has had several career transition talks with his bosses during his decades at the firm. Each time, he got the green light to change course—and a jolt of fresh energy.

One motivator that led him to take control of his career: a health crisis several years ago, when he was diagnosed with type 2 diabetes. "I realized there's a greater purpose for my being here," he said.

(continued)

Today, Johnson's career is a world away from where it was a few years ago, when he spent most of his time roaming around international raceways, consulting with engineers and drivers, and talking to the press about Michelin tires. During Johnson's tenure as head of the company's racing program, Michelin-shod cars took first place at the 24-hour race in Le Mans, France, among numerous other victories, and he was engrossed in the details of racing-tire compounds and tread designs.

Then he navigated a wide turn. In his last position, as chief of community relations from 2007 to 2014, Johnson was more likely to be found lending a hand to build new homes with Habitat for Humanity. Or he might have been meeting with elementary school administrators near his home in Greenville, South Carolina, about a program he spearheaded called the Michelin Challenge Education volunteer mentoring program, which enlists company employees and retirees to provide mentoring in math, science, and reading at public schools near Michelin facilities nationwide.

This year, he's actively taking part in gatherings of Michelin workers who belong to employee groups such as the African American Network, the Hispanic Network, and the "Road to Retirement" Network. A big part of his job is to listen to their concerns and challenges, to develop mentorship programs, and to work to make changes within the organization that will help hold on to great employees. "I don't want them to have to leave who they are in the parking lot," Johnson says.

Changing focus for Johnson didn't mean downshifting to easier work, but it has made the work more fulfilling at this stage of his life. "It's about getting up every morning and knowing I have an opportunity to help someone," he told me.

I asked Johnson about how he went about asking his boss and higher-ups for a switch to his latest position and what he would say to others looking to do something similar. He says he began months in advance by first talking to his human resources department contact about the opening he knew was in the offing to see if he felt it would be a good fit. Next, he sat down with his then-boss to get his advice on the possible transition. His approach was not a direct "ask," he says, but rather a meeting to ask advice and counsel, an approach he finds successful. Here are some of his other insights.

1. *Do your current job to the best of your ability.* "The fact that I did the community job well made the company willing to give me this opportunity."

2. *If there's something out there you want to do, or are interested in, you've got to network.* "It's not important who you know well. What is important is who knows you well enough to have an opinion about your work."

3. *Look at who's doing the job now.* "See if there might be a possible opening in the future somewhere else in the company. I knew that the person who was in the diversity position was closer to retirement than I was, so I had lots of conversations with him about his job. When he announced his retirement, I began to network aggressively to get my name in the hat. I probably started networking for this job two years before I moved into it.

4. *Ask yourself why you want the change.* "For me, I figure I have another five years at Michelin before I retire, and 12 years in one assignment is too long. As an African American, I felt I could make a contribution in the area of diversity. It was something I aspired to."

5. *Check and see what your company's protocol is.* "At Michelin, if you're interested in a change in assignment, you talk to your immediate supervisor. In Michelin's HR department, however, we all have been assigned a "career manager" we work with from our first day at work to build our careers. The company's aim is to adapt to *your* career aspirations and to implement your plan over time. So I consulted with my career manager about whether it was a possible move for me, and how I should get my name into the field of those who were being considered for the position. Then I made it a point to express my interest to others within the organization."

WHAT TO SAY—AND NOT SAY

Here are some sample conversations you might have—and not have—with your boss.

If you want a raise:

Do say:

- "I helped the company increase revenue by X." Or, "when our competitors were stumbling during the sluggish economy, my unit was able to keep sales steady."
- "I've successfully resolved client issues on these three major problems."
- "Based on my work managing the team during the company's acquisition of X, I would like to be considered for a promotion.

Don't say:

- "I need to make more money because I've got to pay my bills."

If you want to make an internal move:

Do say:

- "I see there's an opening in X department and would love the opportunity to learn new skills to help me grow and contribute to the firm."
- "I am interested in learning more about X, a growing area of the firm's business. It's work that I feel passionate about and was wondering if there might be an opportunity to take on perhaps a part-time assignment in that department since I know that Mary or Bob will be out on medical leave for a few months.

Don't say:

- "I'm bored, frustrated, and having trouble seeing how I can advance in my current position."

- "Our department seems to be on the backburner here, and I want to be where the action is."

If you want to upgrade your game:

Do say:

- "I'd love some advice from you on ways I can work on continuing to develop my expertise and career here. Are there any upcoming workshops or skills-development courses offered in the next few months that you think I should sign up for? If not, are there any future classes that you're aware of outside of the company, maybe at an industry meeting or even a community college, that you would recommend I enroll in on my own time?"

Don't say:

- "I know that a few of my colleagues in other departments are being sent to a continuing education program being offered by our industry group. I certainly would benefit from that as well, and I think you should send me, too."

If you want a promotion:

Do say:

- "I would like to move into this position because I have demonstrated X, Y, and Z."
- "I've managed five people and was a key influence on their career development."
- "My direct reports have contributed to the firm by bringing in new clients"—or some other example of how you have directly and indirectly contributed to pumping up the bottom line.

Don't say:

- "I deserve this. I want this. I have put in the time."

(continued)

If you want a more flexible schedule:

Do say:

- "I would like to explore telecommuting two days a week. It would cut out the hour and a half it takes me to get to and from the office. And with fewer intrusions by coworkers, I'd be more efficient. Would you be willing to try a trial period of a few months?"

Don't say:

- "My long commuting is taking a toll on my work. Is there any way I can work from home two or three days a week?"

Chapter Recap

In this final chapter, we discussed a myriad of ways to prepare to have that conversation with your boss about changing some aspect of your job. We walked through how to do your research and networking before you ask for that formal meeting. It takes confidence and the clarity to distill your future work goals to get your boss on board, so take your time to do your homework.

Have a sharp vision of what you really want, a strong explanation of why you're asking, and solid evidence of ways your boss and your employer will benefit from your request. You will also need to hone your pitch before you step up to the plate, so practice it. Plus, it helps to be flexible about what's next. You never know what might pop up once you start the ball rolling. Don't approach the conversation with blinders on.

Your To-Do List

- Distill in your Job Remodeling journal what you want out of your job and how to ask your boss for it.
- Ask yourself if you've really sold *yourself* on what you want.

- Take the time to understand your boss's perspective.
- Write down all the ways your employer will benefit from rewarding you.
- Practice and memorize your pitch. Believe in yourself.
- Be passionate about what you're asking your boss to help you achieve. It's catching.

Afterword

As I was writing this book, I joked with friends that this was my "suck it up" book. And in many ways, that's true. I've spent so much time in recent years counseling and encouraging workers who are struggling to find work that when I meet those who are gainfully employed and hear them complaining about their job, their boss, or their coworkers, I think, *"Come on."*

Stop it. Be a positive problem solver. Dwelling on the negative zaps your spirit and gets you labeled as a "complainer." That kind of reputation clings to you.

Never gossip. Play nicely with others and stay calm and poised, at least for the world to see. You need to manage your career like it's the most important business assignment that has ever been placed in your hands. Do it with grace.

Be grateful—you have a job. Make it work for *you.* If you're unhappy, *do* something about it. You're not a victim. If you really are miserable, quit. But you'd better be sure to have an exit strategy.

Quitting should be the last straw, however. Finding a new job when you are of a certain age can be daunting, as I write about in *Great Jobs for Everyone 50+: Finding Work that Keeps You Happy and Healthy ... and Pays the Bills.* And it takes longer than you can possibly imagine.

Changing jobs or starting your own business can be enormously rewarding, as I explore in *What's Next? Finding Your Passion and Your Dream Job in Your Forties, Fifties, and Beyond.* But that leap is not something everyone can tackle and succeed at over the long haul, for a slew of reasons. For most people, making a career change takes patience, years of planning, and, generally, either enough savings socked away to ride out the early years or a willingness to live frugally. You have to be hardwired for that kind of transformation.

You can, though, take control of the joy you find in your work right now. You're limited only by your own imagination and your commitment to change. If you've finished this book with a sense of possibility and the confidence that you can fall in love with your job again, you're on your way.

You're ready to take this job and *love* it.

As you've learned in these pages, if you're feeling stuck and frustrated at work, you can make changes at your current job that will bring satisfaction and meaning to your work life *and* renew your enthusiasm.

Some of these are big-picture moves—say, asking for new responsibilities or a promotion, or transferring departments. Some are less visible. These are internal attitude adjustments and smart ways of finding happiness around the edges, by mentoring others, learning a new skill, or taking a walk or volunteering alongside colleagues outside the office.

Your assignment is clear. Make a plan. Define what will make your own career path successful for *you*. We all have our own markers for what will propel us forward. It might be a more flexible work arrangement, a sweet salary bump, or a challenging new assignment.

The core message I want you take away from this book is that *you* can turn it around and rebound from your malaise or a grim work environment. *You* have to own it. *You* consciously choose whether to continue being unhappy or pick an alternate path and change it up, even if it's in baby steps. Simply starting on a solution lifts your spirits.

Finding ways to love your job takes time, I know. In fact, these internal career moves work best when they aren't rushed. You never want to be rash and impulsive when you're rethinking your job.

You may have to wait for the right opportunity to arise, but you can start laying the groundwork and preparation right now. At worst, during this initial building process, while you stick it out and still hate your job, you will learn how to work under tough conditions—a good skill to have in your quiver under any circumstances.

I truly believe that most employers want you to be happy as much as you do. It doesn't have to be adversarial.

It really is never too late to find work you love. It's a matter of finding what really excites you.

You might need to get to the point where you realize you're never going to be president and CEO of the company, of course. But when you do find what can really motivate you, you'll get up in the morning and say, "Holy mackerel, I really am excited doing this."

Your homework is finding whatever that sweet spot might be. It's a process.

I would be remiss if I didn't add this caveat: Do make your job one you relish, but don't become trapped by it. As the oft-repeated saying goes, "No one ever wished they had worked more at the end of their life."

A life well lived is all about balance. Laugh and spend time with family and friends, travel, dance alone in your living room to Bruce Springsteen's "Born to Run" when no one is watching—if that makes you feel good. It works for me, but whatever rocks you, just dance. Look around you each day and find beauty: the bright yellow goldenrod in the field, the silent blue heron standing stock-still on the shoreline, the floating cloud formation that looks like it was painted by an artist up there in the blue sky, the smile on a coworker's face when she gets a thumbs-up on *her* work project.

I frequently remind myself of the traditional Navajo prayer, "May you walk in beauty." I send that wish your way with all my heart. Hold it dear.

Build breaks into your workday every few hours for a walk outside, if only around the block. (If you work from home, I hope you have a dog like my Zena to take along with you.) It will keep you healthy, too. Such actions will boost your creativity and help you find solutions and ways to "engage" in your work.

One final piece of advice: There's one basic ingredient for a firm foundation to support the changes you're making. Without it, you may never get what you need to find true happiness in your job.

To turn the tide and move forward with your short- and long-term "love your job" goals, this one is nonnegotiable—*believe in yourself.*

Resources

Ideas for Further Reading

Plenty of great books are aimed at improving your work life. Here are a few I recommend. New ones are always arriving, and I have probably left off a few titles that should be here. But these should help to get you motivated.

The Big Shift: Navigating the New Stage Beyond Midlife by Marc Freedman (Public Affairs, 2012). An inspirational read to help you see why having a passion for your work can make a difference—not only in your life but in the world.

The Confidence Code: The Science and Art of Self-Assurance—What Women Should Know by Katty Kay and Claire Shipman (Harper Business, 2014). Refreshing take on how to make the most of your skills and interests, and ways to ramp up your confidence to succeed in your work and more.

Create Your Future the Peter Drucker Way: Developing and Applying a Forward Focused Mindset by Bruce Rosenstein (McGraw-Hill, 2013). This book uses the wisdom of Peter Drucker to help you create professional success.

Drive: The Surprising Truth about What Motivates Us by Daniel Pink (Riverhead Books, 2009). Enough said. This book will get you pumped about work and life.

The Economy of You: Discover Your Inner Entrepreneur and Recession-Proof Your Life by Kimberly Palmer (AMACOM, 2014). I love this book about finding joy around the edges with side gigs.

The Encore Career Handbook: How to Make a Living and a Difference in the Second Half of Life by Marci Alboher (Workman, 2012). In my review for *USA Today,* I called this book "a practical, energizing, and essential guide."

Evolutionary Work: Unleashing Your Potential in Extraordinary Times by Patricia DiVecchio (Pearhouse Press, 2010). Great advice on bringing passion to your work life.

Executive Presence: The Missing Link between Merit and Success by Sylvia Ann Hewlett (Harper Business, 2014). This is essential reading for anyone who wants to raise their game.

Forget a Mentor, Find a Sponsor: The New Way to Fast-Track Your Career by Sylvia Ann Hewlett (Harvard Business Review Press, 2013). Smart advice on finding a sponsor to push your career in new directions.

How to Win Friends and Influence People by Dale Carnegie (Pocket Books, 1998). This classic people-skills book was first published in 1937 and is still selling. You might also check out an adaptation of it, *How to Win Friends and Influence People in the Digital Age (Simon & Schuster, 2012).*

I Shouldn't Be Telling You This: Success Secrets Every Gutsy Girl Should Know by Kate White (Harper Business, 2012). The former editor of *Cosmopolitan* has written a fun and straight-shooting book for women (and men, too).

The Inner Game of Work: Focus, Learning, Pleasure, and Mobility in the Workplace by W. Timothy Gallwey (Random House, 2001). An oldie, but it never goes out of style. Terrific empowering advice from Gallwey, author of a series of bestselling Inner Game books.

Leading the Life You Want: Skills for Integrating Work and Life by Stewart D. Friedman (Harvard Business Review Press, 2014). A professor from the Wharton School at the University of Pennsylvania offers great advice on finding harmony between your work and your life.

Lean In: Women, Work, and the Will to Lead by Sheryl Sandberg (Alfred A. Knopf, 2013). Shows you how to reach within yourself to create a better work life.

Life Reimagined: Discovering Your New Life Possibilities by Richard J. Leider and Alan M. Webber (AARP/Berrett-Koehler, 2013). How you can find fulfillment in your work and your life.

A Long Bright Future: An Action Plan for a Lifetime of Happiness, Health, and Financial Security by Laura Carstensen (Harmony, 2009). Carstensen is a professor of psychology and founding director of the Stanford Center on Longevity. For more than 20 years, her research has been supported by the National Institute on Aging.

Love 2.0: How Our Supreme Emotion Affects Everything We Feel, Think, Do, and Become by Barbara L. Fredrickson (Hudson Street Press, 2013). Shows how love can transform our lives, even our work lives.

Managing In The Next Society by Peter Drucker (St. Martin's Griffin; reprint edition, 2003). In a series of essays, the revered management guru Peter Drucker discusses trends, emerging industries, and management and sociological changes that can impact businesses.

Me 2.0, Revised and Updated Edition: 4 Steps to Building Your Future by Dan Schawbel (Kaplan Publishing, 2011). Savvy help for shaping your personal brand.

One Person/Multiple Careers: The Original Guide to the Slash Career [Kindle Edition] by Marci Alboher (HeyMarci, 2012). Innovative take on the core of today's work life as we weave together a variety of jobs.

The Pathfinder: How to Choose or Change Your Career for a Lifetime of Satisfaction and Success by Nicholas Lore (Touchstone, 2012). A top-notch bestselling guide to being your own career detective and finding the right work for you.

Playing Big: Find Your Voice, Your Mission, Your Message by Tara Mohr (Gotham Books, 2014). Inspirational ideas to help you take charge of your career.

Promote Yourself: The New Rules for Career Success by Dan Schawbel (St. Martin's Press, 2013). Provides brand-building guidance and ways to ramp it up.

The Purpose Economy: How Your Desire for Impact, Personal Growth, and Community Is Changing the World by Aaron Hurst (Elevate, 2014). How to think more entrepreneurially about your career and look for opportunities where you can make a difference, not just a living.

Pushback: How Smart Women Ask—and Stand Up—for What They Want by Selena Rezvani (Jossey-Bass, 2012). Leadership consultant Rezvani argues that you have to advocate for yourself; women (and men) who don't risk losing promotions, great assignments, and more.

Rebounders: How Winners Pivot from Setback to Success by Rick Newman (Ballantine Books, 2012). Setbacks can be a secret weapon. How people react to stressful events and succeed by being open to new ideas.

Refire! Don't Retire by Ken Blanchard and Morton Shaevitz (AARP/ Berrett-Koehler, 2015). In the trademark Ken Blanchard style, the authors tell the compelling parable of Larry and Janice Sparks, who discover how to see each day as an opportunity to enhance their relationships, stimulate their minds, revitalize their bodies, and grow spiritually.

Roadmap for the Rest of Your Life: Smart Choices about Money, Health, Work, Lifestyle … and Pursuing Your Dreams by Bart Astor (AARP/ Wiley, 2013). Witty and practical approach to working and more.

To Sell Is Human: The Surprising Truth about Moving Others by Daniel Pink (Riverhead, 2013). The bestselling author explains how to really understand someone else's perspective and other insights into getting what you want and selling others on your ideas.

Social Networking for Business Success: Turn Your Ideas into Income by Miriam Salpeter and Hannah Morgan (LearningExpress, 2013). Terrific strategies to ramp up your work life.

Social Networking for Career Success: Using Online Tools to Create a Personal Brand by Miriam Salpeter (LearningExpress, 2011). Step-by-step help with social media coach Salpeter, owner of Keppie Careers.

Stand Up for Yourself without Getting Fired: Resolve Workplace Issues before You Quit, Get Axed, or Sue the Bastards by Donna Ballman (Career Press, 2012). An employment lawyer gives you the straight scoop on workplace issues.

Switch: How to Change Things When Change Is Hard by Chip Heath and Dan Heath (Crown Business, 2010). Who doesn't want to know how to make a winning change? Chip Heath and Dan Heath discuss a common quest in their book.

Tweak It: Make What Matters to You Happen Every Day by Cali Williams Yost (Center Street, 2013). The expert on managing work and life delivers practical, hopeful advice for anyone who is overextended and overworked.

Unretirement: How Baby Boomers Are Changing the Way We Think about Work, Community, and the Good Life by Chris Farrell (Bloomsbury Press, 2014). An upbeat look at how Boomers can navigate this stage of life with a positive outlook.

Your Credit Score: How to Improve the 3-Digit Number that Shapes Your Financial Future, 4th edition by Liz Pulliam Weston (FT Press, 2011). Key advice on getting financially fit.

What Color Is Your Parachute? For Retirement (2nd edition): Planning a Prosperous, Healthy, and Happy Future by John E. Nelson and Richard N. Bolles (Ten Speed Press, 2010). Useful insights and exercises so you can make the best choices for all facets of your life, from work and leisure to health and where to live.

What Works for Women at Work: Four Patterns Working Women Need to Know by Joan C. Williams and Rachel Dempsey (New York University Press, 2014). This mother-daughter duo lay out great strategies to recognize workplace problems and guide your career to thrive at work.

Helpful Career Happiness Web Sites

The number of career-oriented web sites is ever changing. Here are a few I have selected to get you started.

General Information

Following are a few sites, in addition to AARP.org, where you will find a broad range of information on employment and related issues of interest.

AARP.org/work has a complete channel with news, resources, and how-to help (including my jobs column). Go to AARP.org/workresources for guidance in finding a job and AARP.org/startabusiness for starting a business.

AvidCareerist.com is a site featuring tips and articles from one of my favorite career consultants, Donna Svei.

Brazencareerist.com posts interesting blogs from a roundup of career pros.

CareerBuilder.com is an extensive overall career site with articles you might find helpful.

CareerSherpa.net is an advice site from Hannah Morgan, who calls herself a career navigator. While she does dole out job-searching advice, she has plenty of good bits on working on the job you have right now.

Credit.com offers great articles on dealing with your personal finances and information on credit cards and more.

Evilhrlady.org is a witty and straight-from-the-hip site that "demystifies your Human Resources Department," according Suzanne Lucas (@RealEvilHRLady), who runs the site.

Lifereimagined.aarp.org offers an entire section devoted to creating a LifeMap, and more ways to get inspired about your work.

MaggieMistal.com is the site for career coach Mistal, who offers practical how-to videos on asking for a raise and more, as well as ways to take back your career.

Myersbriggs.org offers the well-known personality assessment test.

NextAvenue.org provides timely news and insight for Baby Boomers.

Online.wsj.com/public/page/news-career-jobs. html is loaded with free content for those looking to ramp up their careers. Look for the link to the "At Work" blog.

Pivotplanet.com offers Skype and telephone mentoring for individuals for a fee.

Salary.com is a free source for salary comparisons by city and job.

TheMuse.com is filled with content, but look for the section of articles about career advice.

Tweakittogether.com is where you can find help from Cali Williams Yost, an expert on managing work and life, and author of *Tweak It: Make What Matters to You Happen Every Day.*

Watercooler Wisdom by alexandralevit.typepad.com offers clever career advice from a former nationally syndicated columnist for the *Wall Street Journal.*

WorkOptions.com is a firm that helps employees negotiate for flexible work time.

Volunteering

Droves of organizations offer volunteer opportunities, from your local hospitals and hospices to small community nonprofits in your community. Following are a few large national organizations that can help you track down opportunities in your area that aim to match your skills with projects.

Acp-usa.org is the site for American Corporate Partners, dedicated to assisting veterans in their transition from the armed services to the civilian workforce.

bbbs.org or Big Brothers Big Sisters has been helping children—often those from single-parent or low-income households, or from families where a parent is incarcerated or serving in the military—with one-on-one mentoring relationships.

Catchafire.org matches professionals and nonprofits that need their help, based on a variety of characteristics including skills, cause interests, and time availability.

Createthegood.org is AARP's site for community volunteer projects.

Experiencecorps.org is a national AARP program that engages people 50+ in tutoring and mentoring activities in specific cities across the country, providing literacy coaching, homework help, consistent role models, and committed, caring attention.

HandsOnNetwork.org is the skills-based volunteer activation arm of Points of Light, connected to 250 community action centers.

Hands.org is the site of All Hands Volunteers. It provides opportunities for volunteers to help survivors of natural disasters and communities in need.

Idealist.org provides leads to more than 14,000 volunteer opportunities nationwide, plus internships and jobs in the nonprofit sector.

Joiningforcesmentoringplus.org offers free personal coaching and professional guidance—including working-women mentors— for women veterans of all ranks and eras, military and veteran spouses, caregivers of wounded warriors, and survivors of fallen soldiers.

NationalService.gov is the web site for the Corporation for National and Community Service.

Onlinevolunteering.org is a database sponsored by the United Nations listing online volunteering opportunities with organizations that serve communities in developing countries.

OperationHope.org seeks volunteers with a background in the financial industry to work as virtual volunteers to victims of hurricanes and other disasters, offering financial and budget counseling via the Internet.

NPS.gov/volunteer is the National Park Service volunteer channel.

Taprootfoundation.org places teams of professionals who are doing pro bono consulting with nonprofits. It operates in seven U.S. cities in a variety of fields, including finance, marketing, and information technology.

Volunteer.gov is a one-stop shop for public-service volunteer projects sponsored by the U.S. government.

VolunteerMatch.org allows you to search more than 73,000 listings nationwide via an extensive database of projects that lets you screen for everything from board opportunities to communications positions based on your interests and geographical location.

Continuing Education

Courses offered free online: **Coursera.org, Edx.org, Lynda.com, and Udacity.com.** Search for "free online courses" on Themindunleashed.org.

Encore.org/colleges is a listing of Plus 50 programs at community colleges around the country.

FastWeb.com is a search engine for research scholarships and grants for older students offered by associations, colleges, religious groups, and foundations.

Finaid.org offers resources for student loans and grants.

IRS.gov provides information about educational tax breaks in Publication 970.

Khanacademy.org presents online education courses.

NASFAA.org is the web site of the National Association of Student Financial Aid Administrators.

Osher.net is the home of the Osher Life Long Learning network site.

Plus50.aacc.nche.edu is the site of the Plus 50 Initiative by the American Association of Community Colleges, aimed at students over 50.

Studentaid.ed.gov is a source for information on federal student aid.

Acknowledgments

The creation of a book is a group effort. It takes a team to work together to motivate one another, to inspire, and to construct a final product that has the enduring power to change lives.

Love Your Job was conceived in a brainstorm of ideas one afternoon during a meeting I had with Tara Coates, my astute AARP editor, and Jodi Lipson, director of AARP Books. These two women inspire me on a daily basis by their actions and their words, and I am grateful to have them on my so-called Kerry Inc. board of directors.

Jodi, as is her style, commits to a project and lives and breathes it in her quest for clarity and perfection, and her contributions are considerable and much appreciated on every level of the process.

I am indebted to John Wiley Associate Editor Tula Batanchiev for believing in the book's mission and giving us the time necessary to weave together a work that provides readers the tools they need to *not* take their job and *shove* it, but rather take their job and *love* it.

A shout-out to Judy Howarth, senior development editor at John Wiley, for her deep experience and support in guiding the editorial process with a sure hand.

Edward H. Baker was tossed the editing baton to smooth out my prose and bring some disciplined organization to the flow, and I am thankful for his time and expertise.

A heartfelt hats off to Art Director Lesley Q. Palmer and Creative Director Scott A. Davis, who produced a beautiful and eye-catching book jacket that clearly captures the energy of what readers will find inside.

Acknowledgments

My admiration to my agent, Linda Konner of the Linda Konner Literary Agency, whose support and knowledge of the publishing industry makes her a joy to work with again and again.

On a professional and personal note, Richard Eisenberg, the assistant managing editor of NextAvenue.org, the PBS channel, is not only one of the sharpest editors and creative thinkers I have ever worked with, but he is someone I admire for his intellect and enthusiasm. I am delighted that he is my editor today for my Boomer women and money column, which appears on Next Avenue.org and Forbes.com. Rich and I have worked together since my days as a staff writer at *Money* magazine in the early 1990s, where he was also my editor. And all these years later, we still collaborate and share the road with grace and humor. Not sure what I would do without you, Rich.

And I am indebted to Beverly Jones, an executive career coach, who has generously shared her time and expertise with me for several years and three books. She has become a mentor, a special friend, and, importantly, a fellow dog walker. I raise my glass to you, Bev.

And it's family and friends who bring the ballast to your life. These are the special ones who give you love unconditionally and help you grow stronger along this life journey. Here's to my core crew: the Bonney family—Paul, Pat, Christine, Mike, Caitlin, Shannon—Sassy, and Piper, too; the Hannon family—Mike, Judy, Brendan, Sean, Conor, Brian, my brother, Jack, and his wife, Charmaine; the Hersch crew—Ginny, David, Corey, and Amy; and the Hackels—Stu, Sue, Cassie, and Eric.

For helping me stay in touch with the horse-crazy kid in me and live my passion with my mare, Saintly, hugs to Jonelle Mullen, my trainer, who always finds the time to teach and encourage me, and to my horsey friends at TuDane Farm.

And to my bestie since I was nine years old, photographer extraordinaire Marcy Holquist, who always takes my phone calls.

Finally, my love to my husband, Cliff, for being my behind-the-scenes editorial counsel for more than two decades, and for pushing me to always carry myself with swagger and a smile.

About the Author

Kerry Hannon is a nationally recognized authority on career transitions and retirement and a frequent TV and radio commentator who speaks about and offers advice on career and personal finance trends.

She is the author of the gold-medal award–winning *What's Next? Finding Your Passion and Your Dream Job in Your Forties, Fifties and Beyond* (Berkley Trade, 2014), which *USA Today* hailed as "a road map for those striking out on their own."

Kerry's book, AARP's *Great Jobs for Everyone 50+: Finding Work that Keeps You Happy and Healthy … and Pays the Bills* (Wiley, 2012), is a national bestseller. *The Wall Street Journal* called it "a must read for anyone mulling what kind of work will work for you in the next phase of your life."

Kerry is a columnist for *The New York Times* and AARP's Job Expert and the Great Jobs for Retirees columnist at AARP.org. She is also a contributing writer for *Money* magazine, a contributing editor at *Forbes* magazine, and the Second Verse columnist at Forbes.com. She writes a personal finance column for boomer women at PBS NextAvenue.org, a web site launched by PBS stations focused on America's growing 50+ population.

Kerry has been covering careers and individual career choices for more than a decade. In 2006, she developed *U.S. News & World Report's* "Second Acts" feature—a regular column that looked at people who successfully navigated a complete career change in midlife, their challenges, and their motivations.

She has spent more than two decades covering all aspects of business and personal finance as a columnist, editor, and writer for the nation's leading media companies, including *Forbes, Money, U.S.*

News & World Report, and *USA Today.* Kerry's work has also appeared in *BusinessWeek, Kiplinger's Personal Finance, The Wall Street Journal,* and *Reader's Digest,* among other national publications. She has appeared as a financial expert on *ABC News,* CBS, CNBC, *NBC Nightly News with Brian Williams,* NPR, and PBS.

Kerry is also the author of *Getting Started in Estate Planning* (Wiley, 2000), *Suddenly Single: Money Skills for Divorcees and Widows* (Wiley, 1998), and the *10-Minute Guide to Retirement for Women* (Macmillan, 1996).

She lives in Washington, D.C., with her husband, documentary producer and editor Cliff Hackel, and her Labrador retriever, Zena.

Follow her on Twitter @KerryHannon

Visit: kerryhannon.com

Index

A

AARP, 16, 78
 Day of Service, 78
 Life Reimagined web site, 16
American Corporate Partners
  (ACP), 81–82
"America's Workforce: A
  Revealing Account of
  What U.S. Employees
  Really Think about
  Today's Workplace"
  (survey), 35–37
Ariely, Dan, 8
Armstrong, Steve, 88
Association of Career
  Professionals
  International, 26
Attitude, adjusting, 47–71
 boredom, 48–49
 creating purpose, 49–50
 fitness program, three-step,
   64–70
  financial, 64–69
  physical, 69
  spiritual, 70
 HOVERing, 52–55
 internal motivation,
   improving, 59–60
 journaling, 50–51

 mental games, 57–58
 positive images, 51–52
 workplace bullying, 60–64

B

Berens, Rich, 37
Beyer, Charlotte, 83–84
Big Brothers Big Sisters, 83
The Big Shift (Freedman), 126
Bullying, workplace, 60–64
 Society for Human Resource
   Management (SHRM)
   report on, 60–62
Bureau of Labor Statistics, 2
Burnout, job, 5–6
 medical problems caused by,
   6
 signs of, 5

C

CareerBuilder survey, 90, 147
Career education, 128–135
 affordable options, finding,
   129–132
 cost, help with, 128–129
 educational sabbatical,
   132–135
Careers, switching, 3–6

Center for Work-Life Policy, 80
Challenger, John A., 114
Chesapeake Energy
Corporation, 97
Cho, Eunae, 96
Clark, Jamie Rappaport, 18, 44
Cole, Kat, 121
Conference Board, report by, 1
Create Your Future the Peter Drucker Way (Rosenstein), 77,
125–126
Council of Economic Advisers
report (2014), 106–107
Critical conversation with the
boss, 137–159
carrying out the "ask,"
146–158
flexible work schedule/
telecommuting, 150
moving internally, 150–152
salary discussion, 146–150
sample conversations,
156–158
upgrading your game,
152–155
choosing the time for,
138–140
plan-and-prepare strategy,
142–145
Step 1: What's in it for
them?, 142
Step 2: Play your cards close
to the vest, 143
Step 3: Talk to colleagues
who have made similar
changes, 143
Step 4: Tweak your elevator
speech, 144
Step 5: Schedule a formal
meeting with your boss,
144
Step 6: Make some noise,
145
questions to ask yourself prior
to, 140–141

D

Dattner, Ben, 43
David, Susan, 101
Detweiler, Gerri, 68
Dinneen, Sharon, 76–77
Drucker, Peter, 15, 77, 125–126
Dutra Ana, 114

E

Educational sabbatical, 132–135
Employee Benefit Research
Institute, Retirement
Confidence Survey, 65
Energy Project, 20
"Engendering Inequity? How
Social Accounts Create,
versus Merely Explain,
Unfavorable Pay
Outcomes for Women"
(study), 147
Enthusiasm, as part of HOVER
approach, 54
Erickson, Robin, 152
Ernst & Young, 103
Examining your work and your
life, 29–45
"America's Workforce: A
Revealing Account of
What U.S. Employees

Really Think about Today's Workplace" (survey), 35–37
can-do philosophy, 38–41
choosing happiness, 44
creating a job "budget" sheet, 30–32
determining why you work, 32–34
journal, keeping notes in, 35–41
salary, 38
self-assessment test, 41–43

F

Family Friendly Workplace Ordinance (San Francisco), 107
Federal Employee Viewpoint survey, 2
Fell, Sara Sutton, 109
Financial planners, 67
Fishkind, Ari, 75
Fitness program, three-step, 64–70
  financial, 64–69
  physical, 69
  spiritual, 70
Flexible work arrangements, 99–120
  checklist, 119
  considering, 109–111
  flextime options, 102–104
  laws that encourage, 106–108
  statistics on success of, 104–106
  top companies for, 108–109

work flexibility and happiness, 100–102
working at home, risks of, 111–119
  extended workday, 112–113
  friendships and social networking, lack of, 114–115
  insurance, lack of, 118
  penalty for working later hours, 116
  promotions thwarted, 113–114
  proper business paperwork, lack of, 118
  quarterly taxes, nonpayment of, 118–119
  retirement savings, 116
  tax deductions, 117
Forbes, B. C., 135
Fredrickson, Barbara L., 57
Freedman, Marc, 126

G

Gallup report (2013), 19
Gallup's StrengthFinder 2.0, 43
Gallwey, W. Timothy, 126
General Electric (GE), 78–79
  GE Volunteers of Greater Boston, 79
General Services Administration (GSA), 104
Glick, Leonard J., 58
Global Workplace Analytics, 103
Google, 103
Gratitude, 53
Grunewald Matt, 139

H

Harris Interactive study, 138
Hendrickson, Phil, 152
Hewlett, Sylvia Ann, 81, 84
Hogan Personality Inventory, 43
Hoteling, 104
HOVER approach, 9–10, 52–55
  enthusiasm, 54
  hope, 52
  optimism, 52–53
  resilience, 54–57
    building, 55–57
  value, 53–54
Hurst, Aaron, 49–50
Hynes, Michelle, 92

I

IBM Corporate Service Corps,
  75–76
Ilgaz, Zeynep, 102
The Inner Game of Work
  (Gallwey), 126
Internal motivation, improving,
  59–60
International Coach Federation,
  25, 26
  study (2014), 25
International Labour
  Organization report, 2–3

J

Job description, beyond, 73–98
  adding value, 85–89
  extracurricular activities, 96–97
  renewal, taking time for,
    74–77

time, taking control of, 94–96
  delegating, 95
  interruptions, cutting back
    on, 95
  procrastination, 95–96
volunteering and mentoring,
  77–85
  mentoring and sponsoring,
    80–85
  volunteer work, 78–79
younger boss, working for,
  90–94
Job modifications, 1–13
  finding value in your work, 6–7
  HOVER approach, 9–10
  job burnout, 5–6
    medical problems caused
      by, 6
    signs of, 5
  learning to love your job, 8–9
  switching careers, 3–6
  taking control, 10–11
  taking risks, 7–8
Job Openings and Labor
  Turnover Survey
  (JOLTS), 2
Job Remodeling, 15–28
  adopting new ways to envision
    your career, 24–25
  changing job responsibilities,
    18–19
  creating a job you love, 21–22
  describing your job, 16–18
  hiring a career coach, 25–27
  looking at the big picture,
    19–21
  mapping your future, 16
  work goals, 23–24

Johnson, Herb, 153–155
Joining Forces Mentoring Plus,
    82–83
Jones, Beverly, 16, 37–38, 40, 44,
    48, 51–52, 55–57, 90, 91,
    93, 94, 122
    building resilience, 55–57
Journaling, 35–41, 50–51

K

Kelly Services global workforce
    survey (2013), 88
Krishnamoorthy, Raghu, 78

L

Lawson, Jennifer, 79
Life Planning Network web site,
    25–26
LinkedIn, 139, 147, 151, 152
    "Employees Overboard"
        report (2014), 139
    Global Recruiting Trends
        Survey (2013), 152
"Love Your Job Budget," 30–32
Lucas, Suzanne, 148

M

Mandela, Nelson, 10–11
Marsh & McLennan Companies,
    97
Matos, Kenneth, 150
Mayer, Marissa, 110
Mental games, 57–58
Mentoring and sponsoring, 80–85
    finding a mentor or sponsor,
        84–85

outside opportunities,
    81–84
Michelin Challenge Education
    volunteer mentoring
    program, 83
Microsoft, 103
Mistal, Maggie, 54
MOOC online courses, 129–130
"Morning Employees Are
    Perceived as Better
    Employees" (study), 116
Motivation, improving, 59–60
Myers-Briggs test, 41–43

N

National Career Development
    Association, 26
National Institutes of Health, 97
National Study of Employers
    (2014), 105–106
New skills, acquiring, 121–136
    benefits of, 122–123
    career education, 128–135
        affordable options, finding,
            129–132
        cost, help with, 128–129
        educational sabbatical,
            132–135
    learning and healthy aging,
        123–128
        staying educated, 126–127
        staying relevant, 125–126
        thinking like an
            entrepreneur, 124–125
        traveling, 127–128
    strategic questions, 127
Nyad, Diana, 11

O

Optimism, as part of HOVER approach, 52–53

P

Pink, Daniel, 137, 142
PivotPlanet, 26, 85
PricewaterhouseCoopers, Earn Your Future program, 79
The Purpose Economy (Hurst), 50

R

Rasheed, Komal, 104
Rath, Tom, 43
Redfern, Ed, 134
Resilience, as part of HOVER approach, 54–57
    building, 55–57
Rezvani, Selena, 149
Root Inc. survey, 35–37
Rosenstein, Bruce, 77, 125–126

S

Sack, Mary Ann, 82
Salpeter, Miriam, 91–92
Sandberg, Sheryl, 24
Schawbel, Dan, 22
Schofield, George H., 33–34, 61, 63
Schuyler, Shannon, 79, 102
Schwartz, Tony, 20
Scripps Health, 103
Self-assessment test, 41–43
Skills, new. *See* New skills, acquiring

Sloan Center on Aging and Work study, 106
Society for Human Resource Management (SHRM) report, 60–62
"The Sponsor Effect: Breaking through the Last Glass Ceiling" (study), 80
Sweet, Stephen, 106

T

Telecommuting, 100–102. *See also* Flexible work arrangements; Working at home, risks of
Terkowitz, Roberta, 73, 74–76, 153
Towers Watson global workforce study (2014), 21
Transamerica Center for Retirement Studies survey, 124

U

Unemployment, average length of, 2–3
United Kingdom legislation on workplace flexibility, 107–108

V

Value, as part of HOVER approach, 53–54
Vermont legislation on workplace flexibility, 107

Volunteering and mentoring,
77–85
mentoring and sponsoring,
80–85
finding a mentor or
sponsor, 84–85
outside opportunities,
81–84
volunteer work, 78–79

W

White, Kate, 80
"Work-Life Balance and the
Economics of Workplace
Flexibility" (Council
of Economic Advisers
report), 105
Working at home, risks of,
111–119
extended workday,
112–113

friendships and social
networking, lack of,
114–115
insurance, lack of, 118
penalty for working later
hours, 116
promotions thwarted, 113–114
proper business paperwork,
lack of, 118
quarterly taxes, nonpayment
of, 118–119
retirement savings, 116
tax deductions, 117
Workplace bullying, 60–64
Society for Human Resource
Management (SHRM)
report on, 60–62

Y

Yeager, Jeff, 69
Yost, Cali Williams, 100